Teacher Education, Diversity, and Community Engagement in Liberal Arts Colleges

Teacher Education, Diversity, and Community Engagement in Liberal Arts Colleges

Lucy W. Mule

LEXINGTON BOOKS

A division of
ROWMAN & LITTLEFIELD PUBLISHERS, INC.
Lanham • Boulder • New York • Toronto • Plymouth, UK

Published by Lexington Books
A division of Rowman & Littlefield Publishers, Inc.
A wholly owned subsidary of The Rowman & Littlefield Publishing Group, Inc.
4501 Forbes Boulevard, Suite 200, Lanham, Maryland 20706
http://www.lexingtonbooks.com

Estover Road, Plymouth PL6 7PY, United Kingdom

British Library Cataloguing in Publication Information Available

Library of Congress Cataloging-in-Publication Data
Mule, Lucy W.
  Teacher education, diversity, and community engagement in liberal arts
colleges / Lucy W. Mule.
    p. cm.
  Includes bibliographical references and index.
  ISBN: 978-0-7391-3448-1 (cloth : alk. paper)
  1. Teachers—Training of—United States. 2. Multiculturalism—Study and
teaching (Higher)—United States. 3. Education, Humanistic—United States.
4. Community and college—United States. I. Title.
LB1715.M74 2010
370.71'173—dc22   2010019447

∞ ™ The paper used in this publication meets the minimum requirements of
American National Standard for Information Sciences—Permanence of Paper
for Printed Library Materials, ANSI/NISO Z39.48-1992.

Printed in the United States of America

This book is dedicated to the memory of my father,
George Kang'oyo Ngang'i

Contents

Acknowledgments

There are many people to whom I am indebted for their help and support in writing this book. I thank my colleagues, Rosetta Cohen and Alan Rudnitsky, for providing invaluable feedback on early drafts. I also thank my husband and colleague, Katwiwa Mule, for his support, insightful comments, encouragement, and companionship. My student research assistants, Pamela Cote and Graeham Dodd, were invaluable. Their boundless energy and enthusiasm kept this research alive. I am particularly grateful to the Smith College Committee for Faculty Compensation and Development (CFCD) and the Educational Outreach Office, whose generous support enabled research for this book. Finally, love and thanks to our children—Nyokabi, Mule, and Kalondu—for bringing so much joy to my life.

Chapter 3 was first published in Stephanie Y. Evans, Colette M. Taylor, Michelle R. Dunlap, DeMond S. Miller, eds., *African Americans and Community Engagement in Higher Education: Community Service, Service-learning, and Community-based Research* (Albany: State University of New York Press, 2009).

Introduction and Overview

Recent scholarship contains many proposals on how to reform college- and university-based teacher education to better respond to diversity and other challenges in the K–12 landscape. Data on achievement gaps and other important indicators show that students from low socioeconomic and culturally diverse backgrounds are performing at levels most find unacceptable. Indeed, as many have noted, "both race and social class have a lot to do with whether students will become casualties of school failure."[1] Language is increasingly becoming a factor as well. Responses from teacher education to the crisis in K–12 education have varied, with some scholars advocating stronger links between teacher education programs and content or subject matter departments. Others have argued for the need to ensure program coherence. There exists, especially since the 1980s, a large corpus of literature on the professionalizing of teacher preparation and ensuring alignment with "best practices" based on professional consensus.[2] Others have emphasized partnerships between teacher education and K–12 schools for the simultaneous renewal of both institutions. The literature on professional development schools is quite exhaustive in this regard.[3] Other research points to the benefits of recruiting diverse teacher candidates and the merits of carefully designed induction and mentoring systems for beginning teachers.[4] Yet others have emphasized the need to educate teachers for diversity by equipping prospective teachers with content and pedagogical knowledge, a deep knowledge of diverse learners and their communities, and a critical understanding of the social conditions of schooling.[5]

This book examines the promise of and issues related to preparing teachers for diversity through community engagement. In recent years, the agenda for educating teachers for diversity has become an increasingly important part of preservice teacher education programs across the United States. Almost simultaneously, there has been a growing popularity among universities and colleges of the civic or community engagement movement—a broader movement in higher education emphasizing deeper relationships with neighborhood communities—that gained momentum in the late 1980s.[6] I argue in this book that the nexus of these two trends has important implications for educating teachers, especially in the small liberal arts college context.[7] This book explores the extent to which this intersection can contribute to what I refer to as "community-engaged teacher education," which is used in this book to refer to the concept and practice of linking teacher education and diverse communities for the purpose of educating teachers for diversity. In exploring such an approach, this book addresses several interrelated questions: What is the nature of community engagement in teacher education? What are some of the models that can productively infuse community-based learning experiences in the teacher education curriculum? Why and how should education departments, and the teacher preparation programs within them, form partnerships with community-based organizations in diverse communities? What concrete strategies are useful in forming such campus-community partnerships? What are the pedagogical implications of community engagement? How can a community-engaged teacher education be conceptualized, and what does it take to support it? These questions are important as they bring attention to some of the issues that teacher education faces with regard to community engagement.

This book argues that models of community-engaged teacher education that emphasize collaboration with diverse communities and are geared to the goal of preparing teachers for diversity, while desirable and possible, are often faced with serious challenges. The discussion of these challenges as manifested in the small liberal arts college context is infused throughout the book and provides the backdrop for more targeted discussions that are informed by available literature, my own experiences teaching in a teacher education program in a small liberal arts college for eight years now, and my participation in community engagement efforts at college and department levels. I anticipate that an exploration of these questions and insights will extend the current discussion about the role of community engagement in teacher education reform.

In chapter 1, "Educating Teachers for Diversity through Community Engagement: Reflections on the Small Liberal Arts College," I explore the nexus of educating teachers for diversity agenda, the community engagement movement and the implications for a community-engaged teacher education in small liberal arts colleges. My interest in community engagement stems from the use of service learning pedagogy in my education courses as well as my involvement over the last couple of years in efforts to establish a partnership between Smith College (a private liberal arts college in the northeastern part of the United States) and Hillcrest—an urban, economically distressed Latino community.[8] This partnership has grown in size and importance and now includes a school and community-based organizations in the area. During this time, Smith College has included in its strategic plan a commitment to establish the Center for Community Collaboration, which is expected, among other goals, to provide support for community-based learning. As a member of the working group charged with preparing a report on how to establish the Center, I gained insight into interesting ways that institutional shifts toward community engagement can filter down to faculty and students. I also observed deep institutional anxiety regarding resources, curriculum, and faculty involvement in community engagement. The tensions and potentials relating to community engagement are not unique to Smith College. As I interacted with colleagues in other small liberal arts colleges that are members of the Consortium for Excellence in Teacher Education (CETE), I realized that the very nature of a small liberal arts college presents challenges as well as possibilities for a community-engaged teacher education. In this chapter I use relevant literature and my experience and attempt to answer a two-pronged question: Are small liberal arts colleges critical to the process of preparing teachers for diversity? And, if so, how can community engagement shape their involvement in this process?

In chapter 2, which is titled "Community-Based Field Experiences in Preservice Teacher Education," I examine community-based field experiences (CFEs) as an important component of a community-engaged teacher education. In so doing, I address some of the issues relating to CFEs in education including definition, design, and institutionalization. The term CFE, as used in this chapter, refers to curricular-based opportunities that allow preservice teachers to interact with diverse communities, that is, communities that differ from the mainstream by social class, race/ethnicity, and primary language.[9] Drawing on available literature, I provide a rationale for CFEs in education and outline three categories of CFEs (field trips and brief community inquiry projects; immersion; and community-based service learning/research) in use among teacher education programs, highlighting their pedagogical differences and associated curricular benefits as well as the orientation to diverse communities implied by each. Building on this discussion, I delineate three broad understandings that should inform the institutionalization of CFEs in teacher education: (1) CFEs should become pervasive by integrating them in the curriculum; (2) CFEs should be supported by adequate infrastructure; and (3) CFEs should be aligned to the program core value of educating teachers for diversity.

Chapter 3, "Can the Village Educate the Prospective Teacher? Reflections on Multicultural Service-Learning in African American Communities," delves into some of the issues that may prevent engagement with diverse communities for teacher education. Arguing that culturally diverse communities are an important educational site that has not been optimally used for teacher preparation, the chapter focuses mainly on African American community-based organizations (CBOs) and poses several interrelated questions, the relevance of which resonates beyond the specifics of African American communities: Why is there such little interest among teacher educators to reach out to African American CBOs as sites for community engagement and preparation of future teachers? Why should teacher educators pay attention to CBOs among African American communities? What are the possibilities and challenges involved in using African American communities as sites for community engagement and teacher preparation? How can campus-community relationships involving African American CBOs be strengthened? Answers to these questions are important because they suggest that learning about African American children and providing effective pedagogy for them can be enhanced if teacher education programs strengthen partnerships with African American communities. This chapter also explores the concept of multicultural service-learning in teacher education—including its application in African American communities and other underserved communities.

Chapter 4 is titled "Lessons Learned in the Field about Healthy Campus-Community Partnerships." In this chapter I emphasize that forming partnerships with diverse communities is critical for the community-engaged teacher education programs and their campuses. Noting that the development of partnerships continues to present challenges to many campus-based educators, this chapter discusses the nuts and bolts of developing partnerships with community-based organizations in diverse communities. I describe an emerging college-community partnership between Smith College and the Hillcrest community, and outline six factors that I believe have strengthened this partnership, underlining the lessons that can be learned about healthy college-community partnerships. Taking into account the multiple layers involved for institutionalization, I propose a conceptualization of healthy college-community partnerships as dialogue and emphasize that community-engaged teacher education programs should enter into this dialogue.

Chapter 5, "Community-Based Research as Border Crossing: The Promise of CBR and Barriers to Its Institutionalization in Education," uses the notion of "border crossing," as defined by Henry Giroux,[10] to examine the pedagogical promise of community-based research (CBR). Recognizing CBR as the most demanding among the community-based experiences discussed in chapter 2, I explore ways that education faculty might use it as a means to transcend individual, institutional, and ideological borders when they adopt and adapt it in their research and teaching. Based on my reflections on my work involving CBR, I discuss four options which faculty can use to meaningfully infuse CBR in community-engaged teacher education programs. I also outline some of the barriers that may hinder the institutionalization of CBR in education, and discuss how they may be overcome in the small liberal arts college context.

In chapter 6, "Asserting Community Engagement in Teacher Education," I reiterate the importance of community-engaged teacher education in preparing teachers for twenty-first-century America. I organize the chapter around two questions: Can community engagement really become part of the core of a teacher education program in the twenty-first century? And how should such engagement be conceptualized to avoid the loopholes of past attempts to connect teacher education with diverse communities? I discuss three popular models for connecting teacher education and diverse communities for teacher preparation, highlighting emphases that can be derived across these models. I present a conceptualization of community-engaged teacher education that is based on these emphases and an understanding of influences (program, institutional and external) that have an impact on them.

In this book I have attempted to show why community engagement should become a prominent focus in efforts to educate teachers for diversity. I have argued that educating teachers for diversity through community engagement should be at the heart of teacher education. Without this emphasis, learning about cultural diversity will continue to be considered peripheral in teacher education curriculum. I offer the community-engaged teacher education approach, emphasizing community-based pedagogy through CFEs, and a consideration of institutional contexts. I give explicit attention to issues related to forming partnerships with diverse communities, a topic that has received little attention in the teacher education literature. In my discussion of the community-engaged teacher education approach I have not only considered current literature but also proffered suggestions and ideas derived from personal experiences with community engagement and teacher education.

NOTES

1. Daniel Patrick Liston and Kenneth M. Zeichner, *Teacher Education and the Social Conditions of Schooling* (New York: Routledge, 1991), xiv.

2. Linda Darling-Hammond, Ruth Chung, and Fred Frelow, "Variation in Teacher Preparation: How Well Do Different Pathways Prepare Teachers to Teach?" *Journal of Teacher Education* 53, no. 4 (2002): 286–302; Linda Darling-Hammond, "Constructing 21st-Century Teacher Education," *Journal of Teacher Education* 57, no. 3 (May/June 2006): 300–14; Linda Darling-Hammond, "Teacher Quality and Student Achievement: A Review of State Policy Evidence," *Educational Policy Analysis Archives* 8, no. 1 (2000), http://epaa.asu.edu/epaa/v8n1/ (accessed May 10, 2007); Linda Darling-Hammond and John Bransford, *Preparing Teachers for a Changing World: What Teachers Should Learn and Be Able to Do* (San Francisco: Jossey-Bass, 2005).

3. See, for example, Lee Teitel, *The Professional Development Schools Handbook: Starting, Sustaining, and Assessing Partnerships That Improve Student Learning* (Thousand Oaks, CA: Corwin Press, 2003); Linda Darling-Hammond, *Professional Development Schools: Schools for Developing a Profession* (New York: Teachers College Press, 1994).

4. Alice Quiocho and Francisco Rios, "The Power of Their Presence: Minority Group Teachers and Schooling," *Review of Educational Research* 70, no. 4 (2000): 485–528.

5. Among the notable writers on this topic are Gloria Ladson-Billings, Kenneth Zeichner, Marilyn Cochran-Smith, Carl A. Grant, Marilynne Boyle-Baise, Jacqueline Jordan Irvine, Christine Sleeter, and Anna María Villegas.

6. Dan W. Butin, *Service-Learning in Higher Education: Critical Issues and Direction* (New York: Palgrave Macmillan, 2005); Stephen L. Percy, Nancy Zimpher, and Mary Jane Brukardt, eds., *Creating a New Kind of University: Institutionalizing Community-University Engagement* (Boston, MA: Anker Publishing Company, 2006); Thomas Ehrlich, ed., *Civic Responsibility and Higher Education* (Phoenix, AZ: Oryx Press, 2000); Ariane Hoy and Wayne Meisel, *Civic Engagement at the Center: Building Democracy through Integrated Cocurricular and Curricular Experiences* (Washington, DC: The Association of American Colleges and Universities, 2008); Barbara Jacoby, *Building Partnerships for Service-Learning* (San Francisco: Jossey-Bass, 2003); Carolyn R. O'Grady, ed., *Integrating Service-Learning and Multicultural Education in Colleges and Universities* (Mahwah, NJ: Lawrence Erlbaum Associates, 2000).

7. Teacher education reform researchers have pointed out the benefits to understanding teacher education in its institutional context. See John. I. Goodlad, *Teachers for Our Nation's Schools*; Linda Darling-Hammond, *Powerful Teacher Education* (San Francisco: Jossey-Bass, 2005); Seymour Sarason, *The Case for Change: Rethinking the Preparation of Educators* (San Francisco: Jossey-Bass, 1993); Christopher Bjork, D. Kay Johnston, and Heidi Ross, *Taking Teaching Seriously: How Liberal Arts Colleges Prepare Teachers to Meet Today's Educational Challenges* (Boulder, CO: Paradigm Publishers, 2007).

8. Pseudonyms have been used in place of the real names of K–12 schools and community partners.

9. See Tyrone Howard and Glenda R. Aleman, "Teacher Capacity for Diverse Learners: What Do Teachers Need to Know?" in *Handbook of Research on Teacher Education: Enduring Questions in Changing Contexts*, ed. Marilyn Cochran-Smith, Sharon Feiman-Nemser, D. John McIntyre, and Kelly Demers (New York: Routledge & Association of Teacher Educators, 2008), 157–74. Kathryn H. Au and

Karen M. Blake, "Cultural Identity and Learning to Teach in a Diverse Community: Findings from a Collective Case Study," *Journal of Teacher Education* 54, no. 3 (May–June 2003): 192–205.

10. Henry Giroux, *Border Crossings: Cultural Workers and the Politics of Education* (New York: Routledge, 2005).

1

⁓

Educating Teachers
for Diversity through
Community Engagement:
Reflections on the Small
Liberal Arts College

In recent years, educating teachers for cultural diversity has become an increasingly important part of preservice teacher education programs across the United States. This is true for at least two reasons. The first is related to the changing nature of public education itself: because of the increasing diversity of America's K–12 population, teacher education programs have routinely come to include diversity-focused courses (such as multicultural education, urban education, and teaching English language learners [ELLs]), placements in urban and diverse schools, and community-based field experiences (CFEs) in their curriculum. The term CFE, as used in this book, refers to curricular-based opportunities that allow education students to interact with diverse communities, that is, communities that differ from the mainstream by social class, race/ethnicity, and primary language. These factors are important because they "play a key role in schooling."[1] The second reason emerges from the growing popularity among universities and colleges of the community engagement movement: a broader movement in higher education emphasizing deeper relationships with neighborhood communities that gained momentum in the late 1980s. This increased attention to teacher education reform, community engagement, and the ways in which the two interface is well-documented in the literature. However, as many researchers have noted, the scholarship in this area is typically based on work located in large research-based public universities, and conclusions about ideal models and practices reflect this context. This begs the question: Are small liberal arts colleges critical to the process of preparing teachers for diversity?

And, if so, how can community engagement shape their involvement in this process?

This two-pronged question guides the discussion in this chapter. The chapter begins with an analysis of the agenda to improve the quality of teacher education for cultural diversity and is followed by a brief discussion of key elements of what I refer to as a community-engaged approach to teacher education. I situate this approach in the broader literature on educating teachers for diversity agenda. I examine how this agenda is complemented by the broader community engagement movement in higher education. I explore the nexus of these two trends and the implications for a community-engaged approach to teacher education in small liberal arts colleges. To augment this discussion, I draw from my observations of the small liberal arts colleges that are members of the Consortium for Excellence in Teacher Education (CETE).[2] Like many of the nation's small liberal arts colleges, CETE colleges are residential, private, well-resourced, predominantly White, primarily undergraduate, and small (with 3,000 or fewer students),[3] and their very nature presents challenges as well as possibilities for a community-engaged teacher education. I focus on small liberal arts CETE institutions because they all express a commitment to excellence in teacher education and some of them provide good examples of community engagement work at the institutional level. My reflections on these institutions are drawn mainly from information contained in the CETE colleges' websites, notes taken at CETE annual meetings, a review of institutional documents, and publications by faculty in these institutions. Based on this information and relevant scholarship, I attempt to respond to the question posed earlier.

EDUCATING TEACHERS FOR CULTURAL DIVERSITY AGENDA: SOME FACTORS THAT DRIVE IT

The educating teachers for cultural diversity movement gathered momentum in the early 1990s, and this shift was evident both in the volume and focus of published literature in teacher education. Over the last two decades, an increasing corpus of scholarship—books, edited volumes, handbooks of research, and journal articles—indicate more attention to programmatic structures, institutional contexts, and change strategies for preparing teachers for cultural diversity. Noteworthy among these texts are Liston and Zeichner's *Teacher Education and the Social Conditions of Schooling*; Ladson-Billings' *Crossing Over to Canaan: The Journey of New Teachers in Diverse Classrooms*; Murrell's *The Community Teacher: A New Framework for Effective Teaching*; Irvine's

Educating Teachers for Diversity: Seeing with a Cultural Eye; Cochran-Smith and Zeichner's *Studying Teacher Education: The Report of the AERA Panel on Research and Teacher Education*; Darling-Hammond and Bransford's *Preparing Teachers for a Changing World*; Cochran-Smith et al.'s *Handbook of Research on Teacher Education: Enduring Questions in Changing Contexts*; and Villegas and Lucas' *Educating Culturally Responsive Teachers: A Coherent Approach*.[4] Taken together this scholarship supports a college- and university-based teacher education that is sensitive to the task of teaching America's culturally and economically diverse K–12 population. While there is no consensus on the definition of cultural diversity, in this scholarship it is used to refer to differences related to social class, race, ethnicity, and language. The terms "culturally diverse" and "diversity" will be used synonymously in this book to refer to the intersections of race, ethnicity, language, and class among populations of color. In the literature, the educating for diversity approach is also referred to as "multicultural teacher education," "culturally responsive pedagogy," and "teaching for social justice agenda."[5] The scholarship suggests that the agenda for educating teachers for diversity is fueled by concerns for quality teacher preparation and a need to respond to challenges facing both K–12 education and teacher education. Some of these challenges are outlined below and include: 1) educational disparities or achievement gaps in American schools which often reflect demographics along class, race, ethnicity, and language; 2) a nearly racially homogenous population of teachers; and 3) a narrow teacher knowledge base for diversity.

The persistent achievement gaps in K–12 education not only drive the agenda for educating teachers for diversity but have also become the lightning rod for reforms at the federal, state, and local levels.[6] In addition to test score gaps on state and other standardized tests, other indicators of disparity in educational outcomes include overrepresentation of Black and Hispanic students in special education, lower academic tracks, grade retention, and dropouts.[7] Further evidence of disparity can be found in the allocation of skillful teachers and educational resources. As Zeichner notes, "In every instance, students who attend high-poverty schools, low-performing schools, or schools with high concentrations of African American or Latino students have less-qualified teachers than students who do not attend these schools."[8] Banks et al. point to recent studies that have found that "on every tangible measure—from qualified teachers to access to technology and curriculum offerings—schools serving greater numbers of students of color tended to have significantly fewer resources than schools serving mostly whites."[9] Many teacher educators find racial/ethnic/linguistic/class and other forms of disparities intolerable in a democratic society. As Melnick and Zeichner succinctly put it,

"Although the vast inequities in the U.S. society cannot be attributed entirely to the failure of schools, the failure to provide quality education for *all* students represents a crisis in education that is intolerable in a democratic society."[10] Such educators seek to educate teachers who are not only aware of this crisis and its repercussions on diverse populations but also prepared to eliminate disparities in educational opportunities in their work as educators.

A second factor that influences the agenda for preparing teachers for cultural diversity relates to teacher demographics. Public school teachers are predominantly White and female. Zumwalt and Craig note that "nationally, the teaching force has ranged from 84 to 92 percent White in the past 30 years, with the highest percentages in the mid-1980s."[11] Preservice teacher education programs reflect similar demographics. Zimpher has observed that "the typical graduate of the American education school is female, is of Anglo descent, is about twenty-one years of age, speaks only English, travels less than one hundred miles to attend college, was raised in a small town or suburban or rural setting, and expects to teach in a school whose demographics are similar to her own."[12] On the other hand, as Darling-Hammond observes, the realities awaiting new teachers are different: "In classrooms most beginning teachers will enter, at least 25 percent of students live in poverty and many of them lack basic food, shelter, and health care; from 10 percent to 20 percent have identified learning differences; 15 percent speak a language other than English as their primary language (many in urban settings); and about 40 percent are members of racial/ethnic 'minority' groups, many of them recent immigrants from countries with different educational systems and cultural traditions."[13] It is predicted that by 2035 children of color will constitute the statistical majority of the student population and account for 57 percent by 2050, and that by 2030, 40 percent of the K–12 age population in the United States will be children whose first language is not English.[14] Contrasting this demographic is the expectation, based on predictions of demographers regarding the characteristics of future preservice teachers, that teacher education programs will continue to serve demographics similar to the current ones.[15] The mismatch between a nearly homogenous teaching force and their increasingly diverse student populations is a challenge that many in teacher education urge needs a serious examination of the curriculum and programmatic structures, as well as a development of new strategies.

A third factor that drives the agenda for educating teachers for cultural diversity relates to the desire to develop in teachers the knowledge that will allow them to be effective teachers of *all* students. Howard and Aleman outline the development of policy statements and programmatic efforts to prepare teachers for diversity since the early 1970s when the

American Association of Colleges for Teacher Education (AACTE) first endorsed multicultural education.[16] The goal of this new reform initiative was to garner support for cultural diversity education. Subsequently, other influential bodies in teacher education, such as the National Council for the Accreditation of Teacher Education (NCATE), would echo this concern by formulating a standard addressing this focus.[17] In teacher education, even as programs sought to educate teachers for diversity, the changes became restricted to the curricular, and the approach did not always achieve the anticipated impact.[18] Based on a review of literature since the 1970s, Howard and Aleman note this gap between rhetoric and practice and conclude that, "while there is a pressing need to prepare teachers for diverse learners, issues pertaining to diversity have typically been separated from the rest of the teacher education curriculum."[19] Increasingly, teacher educators who are critics of the status quo have emphasized the need for coherent, institutionalized ways of thinking about educating for diversity, and integrating this thinking not just in curriculum but also structurally in the core values, beliefs, and norms that undergird the teacher education programs.[20]

A COMMUNITY-ENGAGED TEACHER EDUCATION:
SOME IMPORTANT ELEMENTS

Community-engaged teacher education is used in this book to refer to the concept and practice of linking teacher education and diverse communities for the purpose of educating teachers for diversity. This type of focus in teacher education is not new. Zeichner traces the history of this concept to the Flowers Report in the 1940s and to the National Teacher Corps which existed from 1965 through 1981.[21] Other scholars have pointed out that the broader concept of community engagement in teacher education goes even further back to the ideas of John Dewey on neighborhood schools as a social center.[22] The history and fate of past efforts to infuse community engagement in teacher education will be discussed in detail in chapter 6. For now I will outline some important elements of the community-engaged approach in preservice teacher education. The elements suggested here are informed by the work of accomplished scholars on educating for diversity (notable among these are Ana María Villegas, Tamara Lucas, Peter Murrell, Geneva Gay, Jacqueline Irvine, and Marilyn Cochran-Smith)[23] and my reflections, which are discussed in the next section, on community engagement in teacher education in the small liberal arts college context. The community-engaged approach is premised on a curricular focus on diversity and the use of community-based learning experiences. To support this emphasis two related areas must be addressed:

(a) recruitment of and support for faculty and preservice teachers who are committed to educating for diversity; and (b) developing a program vision and institutional infrastructure to guide and support the teaching and learning that connects teacher education with diverse communities.

Curricular Focus on Diversity and Community-based Pedagogy

A community-engaged teacher education exposes preservice teachers to courses that provide theoretical and practical engagement with diverse populations. The goal of such a focus would be to expand the knowledge base for preservice teachers toward diversity. Ideally this would mean that every education course would have diversity as one of the areas of emphasis, and include relevant readings and CFEs. This ideal is of course theoretically comprehensive but translating it to actual practice is difficult for various reasons. For example, many teacher education faculty may lack the knowledge or will to include this content in courses that have previously ignored issues of diversity. There is also the real concern that topics on diversity tend to receive minimum attention in integrated courses, forcing many educators to advocate for special courses focused on various aspects of diversity including language, class, and race/ethnicity. For example, Lucas and Grinberg argue that ELL specific courses are better suited to address particular linguistic issues that are often obscured in courses that focus on diversity in general. ELL specific courses, they emphasize, can more effectively incorporate experiences, attitudes, beliefs, knowledge, and skills for teaching linguistically diverse students.[24] Similarly, others have argued for courses and CFEs focused on urban/rural education and issues of poverty while others have advocated for curricular experiences that underline the saliency of race and racism in education.

Whether in the integrated or single course format the curriculum in community-engaged programs should seek to expand the knowledge base for teachers. Since the 1990s, impressive literature on culturally responsive pedagogy has emerged that has provided conceptual clarity on the knowledge base for teaching diverse populations, including ideology, curriculum, and pedagogy. The concept of culturally responsive pedagogy when applied to teacher education suggests that programs should identify and support the centrality of culture as an interpretative framework in all courses; bring diversity-related courses out of the basement or shadows;[25] develop teachers skilled to support academic excellence of K–12 students; nurture cultural competence in all prospective teachers and help them to "see" with a "cultural eye";[26] develop in preservice teachers sociopolitical or critical consciousness about schools and their social contexts; cultivate in future teachers the ability to use the "cultural characteristics, experiences, and perspectives of ethnically diverse students as conduits for teaching them more effectively";[27] and empower future teachers to teach for student empowerment and social change. Villegas and Lucas summarize these characteristics by describing culturally responsive teachers as those teachers who:

- have sociocultural consciousness
- have affirming views of students from diverse backgrounds, seeing resources for learning in all students rather than viewing differences as problems to be solved
- have a sense that they are both responsible for and capable of bringing about educational change that will make schooling more responsive to students from diverse backgrounds
- embrace constructivist views of teaching and learning
- are familiar with their students' prior knowledge and beliefs, derived from both personal and cultural experiences
- design instruction that builds on what students already know while stretching them beyond the familiar.[28]

While culturally responsive pedagogy's major concern is increasing preservice teachers' knowledge about cultural diversity and its sociocultural contexts, it is also concerned with how this knowledge is taught and learned. Advocates of culturally responsive pedagogy agree that CFEs can provide powerful opportunities for teaching and learning for diversity, especially when they are infused at all levels in the teacher preparation program. An examination of the wide range of CFEs in use in education is the focus of chapter 2. In general, well-designed CFEs are embedded within constructivist views of learning and teaching as they allow for active participation in and with diverse communities and reflection on the experience. Murrell provides good examples of educators working closely with community members to develop educational community-based activities. He argues that such experiences contribute to accomplished practice in urban settings.[29] Throughout this book I argue that engaged programs must (1) reconceptualize the curriculum for preservice teachers to include deep knowledge of diverse students and effective ways of teaching them; and (2) utilize community-based pedagogy as a means to achieve this goal.

Faculty and Preservice Teachers' Commitment to Educating for Diversity through Community Engagement

A curricular focus on cultural diversity and pervasive use of community-based pedagogy is possible when both faculty and preservice teachers are open to community engagement. An engaged program has faculty who are connected to diverse communities through involvement in CFEs, research, community-based program development, and service. Engaged faculty see diverse communities as vital to the development of a knowledge base for educating teachers for diversity and they seek to overcome what Koerner and Abdul-Tawwab refer to as a deep-seated "fortress" culture of the institutions of higher learning.[30] They seek a reciprocal relationship where both campus and community needs can be met and their conjoined efforts help both institutions to participate fully in a democratic society. A lot has been written regarding the urgency to recruit faculty of color in teacher education and the need to offer faculty development around issues of diversity and community engagement.[31] In addition to these more obvious interventions, departments can provide faculty most involved in community-based work with incentives to support their efforts. These may include providing professional development opportunities and supporting the relationships they have developed with community partners. Departments can also encourage faculty scholarship and service that relates to their community work by having this work count toward tenure and promotion. Departments can also support the development of curricular concentrations, such as community studies, urban education, cross-cultural studies, etc., and have courses from these concentrations count toward the education major and/or teaching licensure. Lastly, departments can feature CFEs and other community-based learning initiatives prominently in their websites and/or department/ college newsletters and media releases. This focus on faculty helps validate their work with diverse communities in campus climates that do not readily embrace the concept of community engagement.

An engaged program seeks to recruit the "right" candidates. Recruitment of the "right" candidates is important because of the level of sophistication required to teach today's diverse student population. As Gordon observes, this sophistication demands that programs recruit candidates with the "right reasons."[32] Literature suggests that regular programs can support minority recruitment to this end. In terms of minority recruitment, Sleeter notes that, "neither race, ethnicity, language, or religion determines teacher quality, but a diverse teaching force is more likely than a homogenous one to bring knowledge of diverse students' backgrounds, families, and communities, and commitment to serving diverse students."[33] Programs can also make recruitment decisions that favor candidates who express a commitment to teaching in diverse contexts. In terms of recruiting preservice teachers predisposed to diversity, programs can for example "adopt an admission process that focuses on academic ability 'plus,' which may include dispositions, prior experiences, and bicultural/bilingual competence."[34] To meet the challenge of recruiting the right candidates some teacher education programs prefer to design professional preparation for teacher candidates interested in teaching in schools in poor urban/rural schools or in schools that serve racially and linguistically diverse populations.[35] Such programs attract a more diverse pool of teacher candidates, and have reported higher rates of retention.[36] Whether in the regular program or through special programming, engaged teacher education programs should have a clearly articulated goal to recruit and support the most committed teachers for diversity. Both faculty and students are critical to the success of a community-engaged teacher education program.

Shared Vision for Educating Teachers for Diversity through Community Engagement

An engaged program articulates a clear and shared vision for educating teachers for diversity through community engagement. A shared vision allows a program's core purposes to emerge and, in the words of Hartley, Harkavy, and Benson, expresses "This is who we are."[37] Cochran-Smith provides an excellent example of how programs can develop conceptual clarity around diversity goals. She outlines eight questions that she argues should inform a conceptual framework for multicultural teacher education:

- The diversity question—should the increasingly diverse student population in American schools be understood as a challenge or "problem" for teaching and teacher education, and what are the desirable "solutions" to this problem?
- The ideology, or social justice question—what is the purpose of schooling, what is the role of public school in a democratic society, and what historically has been the role of schools in maintaining or changing the economic and social structure of society?
- The knowledge question—what knowledge, interpretive frameworks, beliefs, and attitudes are necessary to teach diverse populations effectively, particularly knowledge about culture and its role in schooling?
- The teacher learning question—how do teachers learn to teach diverse populations, and what, in particular, are the pedagogies for teacher preparation (e.g., coursework assignments, readings, field experiences) that make this learning possible?
- The practice question—what are the competencies and pedagogical skills teachers need to teach diverse populations effectively?
- The outcomes question—what should the consequences or outcomes of teacher preparation be, and how, by whom, and for what purposes should these outcomes be assessed?

- The recruitment/selection question—what candidates should be recruited and selected for America's teaching force?
- The coherence question—to what degree are the answers to the first seven questions connected and coherent with one another in particular policies or programs and how are diversity issues positioned in relation to other issues?[38]

These are important questions for engaged programs to ask of themselves, and they can help shape the vision toward deep community engagement. In engaged programs such a vision would additionally need to be informed by several important understandings:

- The impetus for community engagement should be a commitment to address the structural inequalities that result in educational disparities along race, class, language, and other forms of differences.
- Teacher education for diversity should involve a combination of university/college, school, *and* community-based activities. Collaboration across these sites is critical.
- Teachers need knowledge about diverse communities, in addition to subject matter expertise and pedagogical knowledge, to be effective. This knowledge should inform both curriculum and pedagogy.
- Community-based pedagogy in diverse communities enhances professional practice. Constructivist views of learning and teaching should guide this pedagogy.
- Community-based pedagogy is challenging to enact and requires certain programmatic and institutional supports.
- Teachers need to understand diverse students holistically as members of the school community, but also as belonging to families and communities with differing linguistic and cultural backgrounds. These differences should be viewed as resources rather than problems.
- Teachers should see themselves as organic members of the communities in which they teach. In addition to their work in the classrooms, they should participate in school-based, after-school, and community-based activities that connect them more organically to the local realities from which their students come.
- Teachers should be agents of change. They should advocate for diverse students (as individuals and as a group) both in school and in the local communities.
- Teachers should aim to teach to broader goals of education, including cultivating critical thinking, attentiveness to diversity and equity, practicing culturally responsive pedagogy, and participation in a multicultural democratic society.

- Schools should seek to advance the intellectual development of their students, while also paying attention to the social, affective, health, cultural, moral, and political dimensions. A holistic approach to education is critical in diverse communities.
- Higher education and community partnerships should be reciprocal. Higher education can join with schools and communities in activities for the common good.

The questions and understandings listed in this section can help teacher education programs shape a "this is who we are" stance that is community-engaged. Besides a shared vision, a curricular emphasis on community engagement and the presence of faculty and students committed to educating for diversity, a community-engaged stance will require that teacher education programs be nested within institutional contexts that support community engagement. The commitment to community engagement at the institutional level is critical to the agenda of educating teachers for diversity. In the next section I argue that the growing trend in higher education toward community engagement can complement the emphases in the agenda for educating teachers for diversity. I explore the nexus of these two trends and the implications for a community-engaged approach to teacher education in small liberal arts colleges.

COMMUNITY ENGAGEMENT AND
THE SMALL LIBERAL ARTS COLLEGE

Colleges and universities across the nation have found in community engagement a unique opportunity to renew the civic mission of higher education and to strengthen and expand the learning and discovery that has been at the foundation of the academy. Faculty and staff are energizing theory, scholarship and research through community collaborations, students are discovering the value of experiential and service-learning, and academic and civic leaders are finding new, mutually beneficial partnerships that unite town and gown in enriching the common good. (Brukardt et al. 2006: 243)

A flood of scholarship starting in the late 1980s indicates that higher education was paying more attention than previously to creating what Percey et al. call a "new kind of higher education,"[39] one that would be more engaged with neighboring communities in addressing local needs while enhancing academic excellence. This trend for promoting community engagement in higher education has been attributed to both policy at the national level as well as institutional support from a committed higher education leadership.[40] Higher education can institutionalize community engagement through incorporation in the mission of the college, infusion in the curriculum, and investment in supportive infrastructure. Important campus indicators of community engagement include: development of campus-wide centers to coordinate community engagement work; involvement of students in a wide range of community-based activities, including community-based learning and community-based research; commitment of academic resources to the needs of marginalized communities; and the integration of community-based work in faculty teaching, research, and reward system. A large corpus of literature now exists that discusses community engagement—its definitions, the structures that support it, the complex process of developing partnerships with communities to support it, its benefits to campus and community stakeholders, and the challenges that threaten it. However, as mentioned earlier in this chapter, this scholarship largely speaks to the context of major research universities.

A look at small private liberal arts colleges reveals that the community engagement movement has also made its mark there, although, with a few exceptions, the mark is nowhere near the repute of major research universities. As Bloomgarden notes:

> [The "elite" liberal arts college] sector on the whole has yet to achieve national standing as a group of institutions where faculty, students and resources are deeply engaged with the community, or as institutions where curriculum, graduates, research agendas, and regional community development are all deeply shaped by this engagement. Neither the grand vision, nor the concrete indicators for a truly "engaged campus" as articulated by numerous scholars of civic engagement are notably in place.[41]

While this critique is accurate in many ways, four areas of promise with regard to community engagement in small liberal arts colleges are worth mentioning here. The first promise toward community engagement is implied in the history of these colleges. Many of these colleges were founded on social roots and their mission statements suggest an orientation that favors community engagement. A cursory look at the mission statements of most CETE institutions reveals that most of them directly or indirectly express a commitment to social justice and/or making a difference in society. Some of these colleges have roots in Quaker traditions and a firm commitment to addressing social inequalities. Others were started to specifically address social inequities based on gender. Smith, Mt. Holyoke, Bryn Mawr, and Wellesley remain women's institutions to this day. Theoretically, colleges with a tradition or mission that is oriented toward social change or social justice are likely to be receptive to the notion of community engagement, although some scholars of community engagement have cautioned against this optimism.[42] To translate mission statements into social justice work on the ground, for example, colleges would require among other things a committed leadership and a comprehensive community engagement plan that is oriented toward helping address the structural inequalities that are suffered by those in marginalized communities.

Community participation of the student body is another area of promise in small liberal arts colleges. Because most of these institutions are residential, they have a strong history of student participation in the governance life of the college as well as community-based volunteerism, which has traditionally served to connect the campus to the community. The reliance on student volunteerism and community service started to shift in the 1990s as criticisms of this model of campus-community relationship increased. Critics see volunteerism as embedded in the highly problematic provider-client mentality that is devoid of social critique, unconnected to the academics, and fails to recognize reciprocity between campus and community. What is of great promise here is the presence of an enthusiastic body of students who despite or because of their being residential can support community engagement in a variety of ways. A discussion group in which I participated at the 2007 CETE meeting focused on community engagement efforts in represented colleges and affirmed the shift away from mainly volunteerism in their campuses. Many agreed that "service in its many iterations is seen as increasingly important to the institutions' missions," and that community-based service learning, research, and partnerships are increasingly gaining currency in these institutions.[43]

One indicator of this growth is the increased efforts since the mid-1990s in some of the CETE institutions to develop centers to coordinate community engagement efforts. I consider the growth of these centers to be another area of promise in regards to community engagement. Centers can help bring institutional focus to neighborhoods and their problems hitherto ignored by the campus. Centers can also influence the curriculum, which is the heart of a liberal arts education. The mission statements of most of these centers emphasize that the liberal arts college is foremost an educational institution, and therefore the justification for community engagement should be linked with the pedagogical. Many in higher education find these two goals mutually inclusive. For example, Swarthmore's Lang Center for Civic Responsibility, established in 2001, states that its mission is "to provide education for civic and social responsibility in a context of academic excellence."[44] Bates' Harward Center for Community Partnership, established in 2002, articulates its mission as "to integrate civic engagement across Bates' educational practices, undertaking programs that simultaneously meet community needs and enhance academic work."[45] Such centers are seen as hubs to organize cross-disciplinary community engagement. The more developed centers make small grants available to develop curricula, courses, ongoing partnerships, training, and other efforts to institutionalize community engagement. As more CETE colleges take up the responsibility of developing similar structures to coordinate community engagement, they seem eager to target the twin goal of community engagement and academic excellence. For example, Smith College has noted that their planned Center for Community Collaboration, "will act as a gateway linking Smith with regional communities and helping students integrate their academic work with community experiences, volunteer service, independent community projects, and Praxis internships."[46] Institution-wide structures such as the ones mentioned above can efficiently develop community engagement efforts in deliberate, purposeful, and institutionalized ways. They can be foci for change and transformation.

A fourth area of promise is the slow but sure attention that community engagement is receiving in academic disciplines. As community engagement continues to take shape in small liberal arts colleges, it is important for academic disciplines to examine how they can support this growth even as they serve their own goals. Bearing in mind that academic departments are the engines of institutional change in small liberal arts colleges, I discuss in the next section how community engagement can complement the ongoing work in teacher education toward educating teachers for diversity.

WHY COMMUNITY ENGAGEMENT IS CRITICAL IN THE PROCESS OF PREPARING TEACHERS FOR DIVERSITY IN THE SMALL LIBERAL ARTS COLLEGE

In making the argument that community engagement can enhance the work of the teacher education programs committed to educating teachers for diversity, I want to stress an observation made by others regarding the important role of liberal arts colleges in teacher preparation. Liberal arts colleges are among the 1,300 or so institutions of higher education that offer teacher education in the country. While they remain a small percentage of these institutions, liberal arts colleges have been identified as important sites for teacher preparation.[47] In *Taking Teaching Seriously: How Liberal Arts Colleges Prepare Teachers to Meet Today's Educational Challenges in Schools*, the authors highlight the strengths that make quality teacher preparation possible. These include the involvement of regular faculty, institution-wide support in the responsibility of teacher preparation, ability to prepare graduates who are well versed in their subject areas and in critical thinking as well as in education studies and pedagogy, and the benefit of strong connections to social justice. These strengths are related to the reputation of liberal arts colleges' success in key areas such as effective teaching and high academic expectations, an emphasis on an education that is both broad and deep, and a commitment to excellence in undergraduate education both in and out of the classroom.[48]

This high-quality teacher preparation in liberal arts colleges can be further enhanced by the infusion of community engagement. Scholarship on community engagement in education and across the disciplines is replete with articles and chapters extolling the academic, civic, and personal benefits accrued by college students from participating in a wide range of community-based activities organized toward these ends.[49] This scholarship emphasizes that the infusion of community-based pedagogy can increase preservice teachers' engagement with course content, enhance participants' civic and social responsibility, encourage innovative pedagogy among faculty, and contribute to the development of quality education for diversity. Teacher education programs that seek to improve the quality and relevance of their teaching through community engagement not only serve their students well but also further the broader tradition of teaching excellence in small liberal arts colleges.

Community engagement can serve to connect teacher education programs and local communities, which complements the professed goal of especially small liberal arts colleges to remain socially connected. Goodlad, in his review of the history of teacher education in liberal arts colleges, has noted that despite the fact that teacher education has increasingly been overshadowed as these colleges expanded and priorities shifted, it continues to be considered by administrators as an enduring expression of the colleges' connection to their immediate community and to social change.[50] As mentioned earlier in this chapter, small liberal arts colleges have recently started seeking deeper connection with diverse communities. Engaged programs that are committed to educating teachers for diversity can help shape this connection in ways that show concern for the structural inequalities that negatively impact the lives and educational experiences of marginalized populations. In other words, the impetus for community engagement in both teacher education programs and their institutions should be social change.

Community engagement allows education faculty to provide courses that connect students to diverse communities and encourage community involvement. A cursory look at the education websites of CETE institutions indicate that some of them include in their listings courses that would be considered diversity-focused. These courses as well as others that reflect more traditional titles include a wide array of community-based field experiences (CFEs). What I found interesting is that many of these courses are also listed on the websites of campus-wide centers responsible for coordinating community engagement, which suggests that education departments are connected to these structures through courses that receive some form of support. The education department at Bates has twenty-nine partnerships through the Harward Center that include schools and community-based agencies and grassroots organizations.[51] Many Swarthmore education courses are listed in the Lang Center's website as having a "substantial community-based element" and are among courses that utilize the 38 community agencies with which the Center partners.[52] At Smith College, education courses such as Urban Education, Literacy in Cross-Cultural Perspective, and Growing Up American: Teenagers and Their Educational Institutions involve students in CFEs in after-school and community-based organizations in low socioeconomic and culturally diverse settings. Some education courses at Bryn Mawr are designated Praxis and are linked to the Civic Engagement Office, which provides logistical support for school and community-based placements.[53] They include Schools in American Cities, Sociology of Education, Arts Teaching in Educational and Community Settings, Multicultural Education, Empowering Learners: Theory and Practice of Extra-Classroom, and Special Education. Similarly, through the Filene Center for Work and Learning at Wheaton College, education courses with school placements and/or CFEs receive logistical support afforded courses designated Experiential Teaching and Learning.[54] Some of the education courses include Multiple Perspectives on Literacy, Schooling in America, Teaching and Learning, and Introduction to Tutoring Writing. The center also supports interdisciplinary capstone courses that integrate field experiences with traditional courses. These examples show that community engagement can positively impact the number of diversity-focused courses in education.

Community engagement can serve to enhance cultural competence among preservice teachers in liberal arts colleges. As noted earlier, liberal arts colleges tend to be predominantly residential, White, and middle class, and their preservice teacher candidates reflect this demographic. Teacher educators are aware that, in order to fully prepare their students to teach in diverse K–12 classrooms, they need to help their students gain exposure beyond their immediate environment and experiences, and equip them with necessary skills to function effectively in diverse contexts. Epstein explains how the need to overcome insularity drives liberal arts colleges to seek closer connections with diverse communities.

The insularity that some associate with liberal arts, as well as the isolated, residential environment that exists within smaller higher education institutions, can create an artificial atmosphere that is not conducive to intimate social and political engagement with groups and communities that exist outside of the campus bubble. It is for this reason that so many national liberal arts colleges encourage extensive study abroad and provide their students with numerous off-campus internship possibilities so as to complement the core set of academic experiences they provide.[55]

To transgress racial, class, linguistic, and geographical borders between prospective teachers and diverse populations, teacher education programs seek to offer courses and CFEs that help preservice teachers increase their accurate and in-depth knowledge of diverse populations; develop strategies for effective teaching of diverse learners; develop critical reflection around curriculum, pedagogy, and the social contexts of schooling; and take action toward social change and social justice in their work as teachers. In this sense, community engagement can be said to be in service of teacher candidates with little exposure to diverse populations.

Community engagement can also help develop deeper faculty connections with diverse communities. A closer look at faculty work in some CETE institutions, drawn from personal communication and faculty profiles and publications suggests that, while organized campus-wide structures can provide direction and support, it is faculty members who develop and sustain the courses, CFEs, research, and programs which strongly link colleges and diverse communities. In some cases, faculty work involving community clearly predates the establishment of centers. From work currently going on in education departments, it is clear that, while not in overwhelming numbers, faculty, either working in collaboration with centers or on their own, are increasingly offering CFEs in their courses and organizing programs and/or doing research that facilitates community engagement. For example, education faculty are involved in direct activities that foster partnerships and deepen links with diverse communities through after-school and summer programming. Faculty are also involved in programming and/or research around urban education, urban and rural poverty, sports and leadership, culturally and linguistically diverse populations, and refugee populations. Faculty work in these areas seems to suggest a growing awareness that educating future teachers for diversity is not simply a matter of equipping future teachers to work effectively with children of color or low-income populations; a critical understanding of how to partner with various community constituents to transform education toward equity goals is also necessary. Faculty willingness to be directly and deeply involved with diverse communities through CFEs, programs, service, and research is likely to further the goal of educating teachers for diversity through community engagement.

Community engagement can also serve to enhance the prestige of education departments within liberal arts colleges. Scholars have noted that engaged education studies or teacher education programs can provide good models that can be used by other disciplines. Epstein has correctly observed that, "teacher preparation programs are among the best and most systematically organized of all types of off-campus study, and their operations provide models for faculty in other disciplines interested in incorporating service learning and action research into their courses."[56] This expertise can only increase as educational reform continues to urge teacher educators to extend their partnership work beyond the K–12 walls to form connections with communities and families from which their diverse student population come. While clearly not the majority, education faculty spend time in these communities, use CFEs in their courses, and some even focus their research interest around their work in communities. As the literature on developing and sustaining community partnerships indicates, faculty buy-in is paramount when it comes to community engagement. Education faculty are well placed to help shape community engagement in their institutions.

In sum, community engagement is likely to support the work of educating teachers for diversity as it allows for the pursuance of multiple goals including helping shape an institutional focus on social change in marginalized communities; serving teacher candidates with limited exposure to diversity through courses, CFEs and other educational experiences; developing deeper faculty-community relationships through pedagogy and research; and enhancing the prestige of teacher education within the liberal arts institutions. All these goals make educating teachers for diversity through community engagement both urgent and possible.

CONCLUSION

Current realities in K–12 education have pushed the agenda for educating teachers for cultural diversity high on the priority list of teacher educators. In this chapter I have emphasized the need to examine the educating teachers for diversity agenda in the context of the broader movement of higher education toward community engagement. I have emphasized that community engagement is important in the process of educating teachers for diversity in the small liberal arts college. These colleges are unique in their professed concern for social change and transformation through curricular and other initiatives. Coupled with the fact that these colleges that serve teacher candidates who are predominantly White are showing increasing interest for community engagement at both the institutional and program levels makes them important sites for educating teachers for diversity through community engagement. I have offered the community engaged teacher education approach as a framework that can be used to promote the education of teachers for diversity in the small liberal arts college. I have emphasized that its important components such as curriculum, faculty, students, and program vision must be aligned with a community engagement orientation. In subsequent chapters I explore further the notion of community engagement through CFEs, focusing on issues that arise for teacher education.

NOTES

1. Kathryn H. Au and Karen M. Blake, "Cultural Identity and Learning to Teach in a Diverse Community: Findings from a Collective Case Study," *Journal of Teacher Education* 54, no. 3 (May–June): 192.

2. CETE is an association of nineteen teacher education programs in selective, private liberal arts colleges and universities located in the Northeast that was formed in 1983 with the goal of improving teacher education in member institutions. The following institutions are members and the small liberal arts colleges among them are in italics: *Barnard College, Bates College, Bowdoin College,* Brandeis University, Brown University, *Bryn Mawr/Haverford Colleges, Connecticut College, Dartmouth College,* Harvard University, *Middlebury College, Mt. Holyoke College,* Princeton University, *Smith College, Swarthmore College,* University of Pennsylvania, *Vassar College, Wellesley College, Wheaton College,* and Yale University. See http://www.princeton.edu/~tprep/cete/members.htm.

3. For detailed discussions on the features of small liberal arts colleges, see Steven R. Timmermans and Jeffrey P. Bouman, "Seven Ways of Teaching and Learning: University-Community Partnerships at Baccalaureate Institutions," *Journal of Community Practice* 2, nos. 3 and 4 (2005): 89–101; Gregory Prince, "A Liberal Arts College Perspective," in *Civic Responsibility and Higher Education,* ed. Thomas Ehrlich (Phoenix: Oryx Press, 2000), 249–62; Alan H. Bloomgarden, "Civic Engagement and the 'Research College,'" *Journal of Metropolitan Universities* 18, no. 1 (2007): 56–67; Irving Epstein, "Standardization and Its Discontents: The Standards Movement and Teacher Education in the Liberal Arts College Environment," in *Taking Teaching Seriously: How Liberal Arts Colleges Prepare Teachers to Meet Today's Educational Challenges,* ed. Christopher Bjork, D. Kay Johnston, and Heidi Ross (Boulder, CO: Paradigm Publishers, 2007), 31–50.

4. Additional noteworthy texts include Ken Zeichner, Susan Melnick, and Mary Louise Gomez, eds., *Currents of Reform in Preservice Teacher Education* (New York: Teachers College Press, 1996); Joyce E. King, Etta R. Hollins, and Warren C. Hayman, eds., *Preparing Teachers for Cultural Diversity* (New York: Teachers College Press, 1997); Leonard Kaplan and Roy Eldefelt, eds., *Teachers for the New Millennium: Aligning Teacher Development, National Goals, and High Standards for All Students* (Thousand Oaks, CA: Corwin Press, 1996); Christopher Bjork, D. Kay Johnston, and Heidi Ross, ed. *Taking Teaching Seriously: How Liberal Arts Colleges Prepare Teachers to Meet Today's Educational Challenges;* and Linda Darling-Hammond, *Powerful Teacher Education* (San Francisco: Jossey-Bass, 2005).

5. See Ken Zeichner, "Reflections of a University-Based Teacher Educator on the Future of College- and University-Based Teacher Education," *Journal of Teacher Education* 57, no. 3 (2006): 326–40; Marilyn Cochran-Smith, "The Multiple

Meanings of Multicultural Teacher Education"; Geneva Gay, "Preparing for Culturally Responsive Teaching."

6. For example, a major goal of the federal No Child Left Behind legislation is "to improve the academic performance of all students, while simultaneously closing the achievement gaps that persist between students from different ethnic groups and economic backgrounds." See National Collaborative on Diversity in the Teaching Force, "Assessment of Diversity in America's Teaching Force. A Call to Action," in *Handbook of Research on Teacher Education*, 501.

7. Ann María Villegas and Danné E. Davis, "Preparing Teachers of Color to Confront Racial/Ethnic Disparities in Educational Outcomes," in *Handbook of Research on Teacher Education: Enduring Questions in Changing Contexts*, ed. Marilyn Cochran-Smith, Sharon Feiman-Nemser, D. John McIntyre, and Kelly Demers (New York: Routledge & Association of Teacher Educators, 2008), 583–605.

8. Kenneth M. Zeichner, "The Adequacies and Inadequacies of Three Current Strategies to Recruit, Prepare, and Retain the Best Teachers for All Students," *Teachers College Record* 105, no. 3 (2003): 496.

9. James Banks et al., "Teaching Diverse Learners," in *Preparing Teachers for a Changing World*, ed. Linda Darling-Hammond and John Bransford (San Francisco: Jossey-Bass, 2005), 238. See also Alan Vanneman, Linda Hamilton, Janet Baldwin Anderson, Taslima Rahman, "Achievement Gaps: How Black and White Students in Public Schools Perform in Mathematics and Reading on the National Assessment of Educational Progress," http://nces.ed.gov/nationsreportcard/pubs/studies/2009455.asp (accessed July 24, 2009).

10. Susan L. Melnick and Kenneth M. Zeichner, "Teacher Education's Responsibility to Address Diversity Issues: Enhancing Institutional Capacity," in *Preparing Teachers for Cultural Diversity*, ed. Joyce E. King, Etta R. Hollins, Warren C. Hayman (New York: Teachers College Press, 1997), 23.

11. Karen Zumwalt and Elizabeth Craig, "Who Is Teaching? Does It Matter?" in *Handbook of Research on Teacher Education*, 411.

12. Nancy L. Zimpher, "Right-Sizing Teacher Education: The Policy Imperative," in *Teachers for the New Millennium: Aligning Teacher Development, National Goals, and High Standards for All Students*, ed. Leonard Kaplan and Roy A. Edelfelt (Thousand Oaks, CA: Corwin Press, 1996), 51.

13. Linda Darling-Hammond, "Constructing 21st-Century Teacher Education," *Journal of Teacher Education* 57, no. 3 (May/June 2006): 300–14.

14. Etta Hollins and Maria Torres Guzman, "Research on Preparing Teachers for Diverse Populations," in *Studying Teacher Education: The Report of the AERA Panel on Research and Teacher Education*, ed. Marilyn Cochran-Smith and Kenneth M. Zeichner (Mahwah, NJ: Lawrence Erlbaum Associates, 2005), 478; AACTE (2002) quoted in Tamara Lucas and Jaime Grinberg, "Responding to the Linguistic Reality of Mainstream Classrooms: Preparing All Teachers to Teach English Language Learners," in *Handbook of Research on Teacher Education*, 608.

15. National Collaborative on Diversity in the Teaching Force, "Assessment of Diversity in America's Teaching Force. A Call to Action," in *Handbook of Research on Teacher Education*, 501–7.

16. Tyrone Howard and Glenda R. Aleman, "Teacher Capacity for Diverse Learners," 157.

17. Jacqueline Jordan Irvine, "Diversity and Teacher Education: People, Pedagogy, and Politics," in *Handbook of Research on Teacher Education*, 675–78.

18. Literature contains many studies that report beginning teachers' feelings of unpreparedness with regard to diverse population. See for example, Lucas and Grinberg, "Responding to the Linguistic Reality of Mainstream Classrooms," in *Handbook of Research on Teacher Education*, 606–36.

19. Tyrone Howard and Glenda R. Aleman, "Teacher Capacity for Diverse Learners: What Do Teachers Need to Know?" in *Handbook of Research on Teacher Education*, 157.

20. Jacqueline Jordan Irvine, *Educating Teachers for Diversity: Seeing with a Cultural Eye* (New York: Teachers College Press, 2003); Ana María Villegas and Tamara Lucas, "Responding to the Linguistic Reality of Mainstream Classrooms"; Ana María Villegas and Tamara Lucas, *Educating Culturally Responsive Teachers: A Coherent Approach* (Albany: Sate University of New York Press, 2002); Peter Murrell, *The Community Teacher: A New Framework for Effective Urban Teaching* (New York: Teachers College Press, 2001); and Marilyn Cochran-Smith, "The Multiple Meanings of Multicultural Teacher Education"; Jacqueline Jordan Irvine, *Educating Teachers for Diversity*; and Geneva Gay, "Preparing for Culturally Responsive Teaching."

21. Kenneth Zeichner, "Introduction: Settings for Teacher Education," in *Handbook of Research on Teacher Education*, 263–68.

22. Lee Benson, Ira Harkavy, and John Puckett, *Dewey's Dream: Universities and Democracies in an Age of Education Reform: Civil Society, Public Schools, and Democratic Citizenship* (Philadelphia, PA: Temple University Press, 2007).

23. Ana María Villegas and Tamara Lucas, "Responding to the Linguistic Reality of Mainstream Classrooms"; Ana María Villegas and Tamara Lucas, *Educating Culturally Responsive Teachers: A Coherent Approach*; Peter Murrell, *The Community Teacher: A New Framework for Effective Urban Teaching*; Marilyn Cochran-Smith, "The Multiple Meanings of Multicultural Teacher Education"; Jacqueline Jordan Irvine, *Educating Teachers for Diversity*; and Geneva Gay, "Preparing for Culturally Responsive Teaching."

24. Tamara Lucas and Jaime Grinberg, "Responding to the Linguistic Reality of Mainstream Classrooms."

25. Sonia Nieto, "Bringing Bilingual Education Out of the Basement, and Other Imperatives for Teacher Education," in *Lifting Every Voice: Pedagogy and Politics of Bilingualism*, ed. Zeynep F. Beykont (Cambridge, MA: Harvard Education Pub. Group, 2000), 187–207; Tamara Lucas and Jaime Grinberg, "Responding to the Linguistic Reality of Mainstream Classrooms."

26. Jacqueline Jordan Irvine, *Educating Teachers for Diversity*.

27. Geneva Gay, "Preparing for Culturally Responsive Teaching," *Journal of Teacher Education* 53, no. 2 (2002): 106–17.

28. All six bulleted items are quoted directly from Ana María Villegas and Tamara Lucas, *Educating Culturally Responsive Teachers*, xiv.

29. Peter Murrell, *The Community Teacher*.

30. Mari Koerner and Najwa Abdul-Tawwab, "Using Community as a Resource for Teacher Education: A Case Study," *Equity & Excellence in Education* 39 (2006): 37–46.

31. See Ana María Villegas and Tamara Lucas, *Educating Culturally Responsive Teachers;* Susan L. Melnick and Kenneth M. Zeichner, "Teacher Education's Responsibility to Address Diversity."

32. June A. Gordon, *The Color of Teaching* (New York: Routledge and Falmer, 2000).

33. Christine Sleeter, "Equity, Democracy, and Neoliberal Assaults on Teacher Education," *Teaching and Teacher Education* 24 (2008b): 1947–57.

34. Christine Sleeter, "Equity, Democracy."

35. For examples, see Christine Sleeter, "Equity"; Gloria Ladson-Billings, *Crossing Over to Canaan: The Journey of New Teachers in Diverse Classrooms* (San Francisco, CA: Jossey-Bass, 2001); Ann María Villegas and Danné E. Davis, "Preparing."

36. Christine Sleeter, "Equity, Democracy, and Neoliberal Assaults on Teacher Education," *Teaching and Teacher Education* 24 (2008) 1947–57.

37. Matthew Hartley, Ira Harkavy and Lee Benson, "Putting Down Roots in the Groves of Academe: The Challenges of Institutionalizing Service-Learning," in *Service-Learning in Higher Education: Critical Issues and Directions,* ed. Dan W. Butin (New York: Palgrave Macmillan, 2005), 205–22.

38. All eight bulleted items are quoted directly from Marilyn Cochran-Smith, "The Multiple Meanings of Multicultural Teacher Education," 7–26.

39. Stephen Percy, Nancy Zimpher and Mary Jane Brukardt, eds., *Creating a New Kind of University: Institutionalizing Community-University Engagement* (Boston, MA: Anker Publishing Company, Inc., 2006), 242–61.

40. At the national level, the U.S. Department of Housing and Urban Development (HUD) established the Office of University Partnerships (OUP) in 1994, which in turn set up the Community Outreach Partnership Centers (COPC) program. The goal of OUP, as is stated on their website, is "to encourage and fund institutions of higher education to undertake community development activities." Higher education leadership that has contributed to the community engagement movement is evident in coalitions and organizations such as The Coalition of Urban and Metropolitan Universities and Campus Compact. According to their website, Campus Compact, formed in 1985, was forged by college and university presidents and continues to provide material support and leadership to enhance civic engagement in higher education. Similarly, the mission of the public and private universities in the Coalition of Urban and Metropolitan Universities is to strive for academic excellence while contributing to the economic development, social health, and cultural vitality of the urban or metropolitan centers served. See http://www.oup.org/; http://www.cumuonline.org/; http://www.compact.org/

41. Bloomgarden, "Civic Engagement," 57.

42. For example, David J. Maurrasse cautions that missions are often rhetorical and that "sometimes talk is just talk." See *Beyond the Campus: How Colleges and Universities Form Partnerships with Their Communities* (New York: Routledge, 2001), 6.

43. Minutes of the CETE Annual Meeting, 2007.

44. See http://www.swarthmore.edu/x16049.xml (accessed May 16, 2009).

45. See http://www.bates.edu/x171616.xml (accessed May 20, 2009).

46. See http://www.smith.edu/future/design/collaboration.php (accessed June 15 2009).

47. Ken Zeichner, "Reflections," 330.

48. See Ernest T. Pascarella et al., "Do Liberal Arts Colleges Really Foster Good Practices in Undergraduate Education?" *Journal of College Student Development* 45, no. 1 (2004): 57–74.

49. See, among others, Carolyn R. O'Grady ed., *Integrating Service-Learning and Multicultural Education in Colleges and Universities* (Mahwah, NJ: Lawrence Erlbaum Associates, 2000); Joseph Erickson and Jeffery B. Anderson, eds., *Learning with the Community: Concepts and Models for Service-Learning in Teacher Education* (Sterling, VA: Stylus Publishing, LLC, 2005).

50. John. I Goodlad, *Teachers for Our Nation's Schools* (San Francisco, CA: Jossey-Bass, 1990).

51. See http://www.bates.edu/x171616.xml (accessed May 20, 2009).

52. See http://www.swarthmore.edu/x16049.xml (accessed May 16, 2009).

53. http://www.brynmawr.edu/ceo/programs/praxis/courses.html (accessed July 25 2009).

54. http://wheatoncollege.edu/Filene/Faculty/courses.html (accessed May 26, 2009).

55. Irving Epstein, "Standardization and Its Discontents," 43.

56. Irving Epstein, "Standardization and Its Discontents," 43.

2

Community-Based Field Experiences in Preservice Teacher Education

In chapter 1, I introduced the concept of community-engaged teacher education and emphasized a curricular focus on diversity as one of its key features with CFEs as an important part of this curriculum. But what are CFEs, and how do they aid in the process of preparing teachers for diversity through community engagement? This question brings attention to issues relating to definition, design, and institutionalization of CFEs in teacher education. In this chapter, I provide a rationale for infusing CFEs in teacher education and argue for their institutionalization. Using the definition of CFEs provided in chapter 1, as curricular-based opportunities that allow preservice teachers to interact with diverse communities, my discussion excludes field experiences that are confined to K–12 classroom events only, but includes those that emphasize both classroom and community involvement. CFEs may take the form of long-term immersion or moderate to short term, less intensive visits to communities and community-based organizations or agencies. Drawing on the literature, I outline three categories of CFEs (field trips and brief community inquiry projects; immersion; and service-learning) in use among teacher education programs, highlighting their pedagogical differences and associated curricular benefits as well as the faculty perspective(s) on community engagement implied by each. Returning to the discussion on the community-engaged teacher education program, I delineate three areas that are critical for the institutionalization of CFEs.

WHY INFUSE COMMUNITY-BASED
FIELD EXPERIENCES IN TEACHER EDUCATION?

There are many reasons for incorporating CFEs in teacher education programs and education studies. Some relate to such imperatives facing K–12 education as the achievement gap, opportunity gap, dropouts, and home-school cultural gaps.[1] Others derive from the enduring challenges facing teacher education programs of preparing quality teachers for diversity. Teacher education programs continue to struggle with ways to prepare a predominantly White, middle-class teaching force to teach an increasingly diverse K–12 population. Over the last few decades in response to concerns about changing demographics in K–12 populations, growing educational disparities that are mapped along the lines of economic, linguistic, and cultural differences, and a teaching force that does not feel well prepared to teach diverse populations, the attention to the knowledge base for teaching for diversity, i.e., knowledge, understanding, skills, and dispositions, of today's teachers has drastically increased.[2]

The need to improve the knowledge base of future teachers of diverse populations has been acknowledged by various stakeholders, including teacher education organizations such as American Association of Colleges for Teacher Education (AACTE) and Association of Teacher Educators (ATE), accrediting bodies (e.g., NCATE), government (at national and state levels), and teacher education scholars. The National Council for the Accreditation of Teacher Education, for instance, correctly observes, "American society is becoming more diverse, with students in classrooms drawn from many cultures and ethnic groups. Preparing teachers to teach all students to meet society's demands for high performance has created a new agenda for educators and policymakers. To meet these changing needs, norms in teacher preparation and licensing are changing."[3]

The new norms toward preparing effective teachers for diversity include diversity specific courses, school-based placements, and CFEs targeted at increasing the knowledge about diverse students—as individuals, their lived experiences, their families as well as their communities and their "funds of knowledge." Grant and Gillette[4] conceptualize the knowledge base for an effective teacher for diversity in six overlapping domains: culturally responsive teaching; self knowledge; well constructed philosophy of education; pedagogical content knowledge; educational psychology that is multicultural; and connecting teacher education to the world outside the school. Regarding the latter they observe, "The extent to which candidates are involved in the community and use community resources in their clinical experiences speaks volumes about their commitment to the school and to the students" (p. 296). Grant and Gillette are among many advocates of an expanded knowledge base in teacher education who see CFEs as playing a critical role in overcoming the shortcomings of teacher education for diversity. Among the commonly cited strengths of CFEs is their ability to help preservice teachers increase their diversity awareness; deepen their social responsibility and civic engagement; deepen their awareness of the multiplicity of factors that inform the educational process; gain a better understanding of the sociocultural contexts of K–12 students; and identify, locate, and make use of community assets in their teaching. Cairn and Wegener, emphasizing the centrality of CFEs in the teacher preparation process, even go further and argue that "a broader understanding of learning, teaching, and knowledge encountered through participation in varied [community] settings may prompt the revision, reconstruction, and redefinition of schools and schooling."[5] This sentiment is echoed by Koerner and Abdul-Tawwab,[6] who argue that linking teacher education programs with diverse families and communities would eventually enhance K–12 education. Similarly, Myers and Pickeral have argued that preservice teachers whose education is linked with communities are likely to use community engagement to inform their pedagogy as well as develop "the skills needed to contribute significantly to broad-based school reform."[7] The argument by these authors is that with careful education preservice teachers can successfully educate all students and act as powerful change agents in K–12 education. CFEs are an important part of this preservice teacher education.

But how does a teacher education program amid the array of competing demands infuse in its curriculum field experiences that focus on especially low-income and linguistically and culturally diverse communities? How can CFEs be institutionalized in teacher education programs? The discussion in the next section addresses the first question by clarifying the range of community-based field experiences utilized in education.

COMMUNITY-BASED FIELD EXPERIENCES IN EDUCATION

Most teacher preparation takes place through a four-year undergraduate program that combines academic courses and professional studies. Some schools enroll students who have completed a bachelor's degree program in a fifth year program that focuses exclusively on professional studies. Other schools operate one- or two-year programs where students with a bachelor's degree can gain a master's in teaching and/or licensure. The program of study for most undergraduate preservice teachers is similar. During the first two years of college, they complete their general requirements and in some cases begin to take education courses. They take a mix of courses in the subject matter fields they wish to teach, as well as arts and science courses to provide a broad base of knowledge. The third and fourth year comprise a professional concentration that includes foundation courses in such areas as the historical, philosophical, and sociological studies of education as well as human development and educational psychology courses. Also included as part of professional preparation are special education courses, methods of teaching courses, school-based, and sometimes community-based, pre-student teaching field experiences, and the student teaching practicum. Increasingly departments of education are also offering social and cultural diversity specific courses such as multicultural education, teaching of ELL courses, and urban education courses.

The literature review that informs this chapter focused on studies on education courses with CFEs for two reasons: one, to examine the range of CFEs in use in teacher education programs; and two, to explore factors that may facilitate the institutionalization of CFEs in education. To capture the range of CFEs in use in education, the literature review was organized around six areas that concern teacher educators interested in the integration of CFEs in their courses and/or program: (1) type of CFE and degree of integration in an education course; (2) whether on not the CFE was linked to prior field experiences; (3) types of students' activities while in community sites; (4) types of structured reflection; and (5) reported curricular benefits of the CFE. The literature revealed three broad categories of CFEs in education: field trips and/or brief community inquiry projects; cultural immersion; and service-learning. As will become clear in my discussion in the next section, all three differ with regard to the five factors mentioned above. It is therefore important to grasp the nuances of each of these categories. However, while these differences are important, it is the community engagement perspective[8] that faculty bring into the design of CFEs that can support preservice teachers in a complex understanding of, and participation in, diverse communities in the process of their education. I return to a discussion of faculty perspectives of CFEs in a later section.

With regard to institutionalization of CFEs in education departments or programs, few of the studies reviewed gave a sense of if and how CFEs were institutionalized in the teacher education program. Judging from the studies reviewed, the institutionalization of CFEs has not received the scholarly attention it deserves. A similar conclusion was reached by Anderson and Erickson in their survey of a national sample of teacher education programs that sought to gain a deeper understanding of the status of service-learning in the curriculum of preservice teacher education programs. Their findings suggested a "rather broad but shallow penetration of service-learning into the curricula of U.S. teacher education institutions."[9] The term institutionalization is used in this chapter following the definition by Elkholm and Trier, who define it as "a developmental process that appears during and after the implementation of an innovation [and] is used in a routine manner . . . accepted by the users as something normal that is expected to continue."[10] According to this definition, if we take CFEs to be an innovation in teacher education then they would become institutionalized when they are accepted by faculty and preservice teachers and routinely used. Hartley, Harkavy, and Benson emphasize that infrastructure and vision are equally important in institutionalization. They note that an innovation is considered fully institutionalized when it is "found throughout the organization, is supported by adequate structures, and is viewed widely as expressing core institutional [i.e. departmental] values." In other words, it expresses "This is who we are."[11] These definitions suggest that institutionalization means embedding CFEs broadly and deeply in education in order to ensure sustainability and thus success. An in-depth discussion of the institutionalization of CFEs in teacher education programs is necessary, especially as it relates to the process of preparing teachers for diversity. I return to this discussion later on in the chapter.

All the studies reviewed for this chapter examined education courses focused on the preparation of teachers for diverse population including students from low-income backgrounds, language minorities, students of color, and those from urban or rural contexts. In each, CFEs were considered important in the process of preparing teachers for diversity. Following the approach adopted by Hollins and Guzman,[12] the review concentrated on studies published in reputable teacher education journals including *Journal of Teacher Education, Action in Teacher Education, Equity and Excellence in Education,* and *Teaching and Teacher Education.* Also reviewed were cases reported in notable teacher education research handbooks, reports, and edited books such as *Studying Teacher Education: The Report of the AERA Panel on Research and Teacher Education; Preparing Teachers for a Changing World: Powerful Teacher Education;* and *Funds of Knowledge: Theorizing Practices in Households, Communities, and Classrooms.* Focusing on studies that were published between 2000 and 2008, the search yielded a total of thirty-five studies, a somewhat disappointing yield but one that was not unexpected. Other researchers have noted the scarcity of studies focusing on CFEs.[13] With few exceptions, the bulk of the studies reviewed focused on small-scale studies conducted in individual courses, often by the instructors. Taken together, the studies reviewed for this chapter seemed to suggest that the various iterations of CFEs are useful in teacher education. They help preservice teacher to: increase diversity awareness; analyze and overcome preconceived notions of diverse students; gain an appreciation of student cultural and linguistic diversity; gain a better understanding of the sociocultural needs of K–12 students; provide service to communities in need; learn how to identify and make

use of community assets; grasp the notion of culturally responsive pedagogy; deepen their understanding of the connection between cultural
diversity, racism, and educational issues; develop stronger ethnic identity
and commitment to teaching for social justice; increase their interest for
teaching in diverse settings and/or using CFEs in their classroom practice; and develop a "community engaged orientation."[14] However, the
studies suggest a general caution that, when poorly organized, CFEs can
lead to preservice teachers generating negative beliefs about teaching in
culturally diverse contexts.[15] This caution should be taken seriously by
education faculty as they design CFEs, especially if their goal is to develop in preservice teachers a complex understanding of, and participation in, diverse communities.

TYPES OF COMMUNITY-BASED
FIELD EXPERIENCES IN EDUCATION

The literature revealed three broad categories of CFEs in education:
field trips and/or community inquiry projects; cultural immersion; and
service-learning. The three categories help illustrate the various ways
education faculty infuse CFEs in their course. All three categories differ
in terms of degree of integration in education courses, time commitment,
nature of student activities, types of structured reflection, reported curricular benefits, and faculty perspective on community engagement. Each
category is briefly described below.

Field Trips and/or Brief Community Inquiry Projects

Field trips, neighborhood tours, or community plunges are common in
educational foundation courses and specialized courses on linguistic/
cultural diversity and urban/rural education. Field trips include brief visits to the community, usually a few hours to a day. Students may simply
take a walk through the neighborhood, visit community sites, observe in
community programs, eat in a local restaurant, or meet with key community leaders to learn simple facts about the community. They may even
make follow up visits to meet and talk with residents. Sometimes, they
may shadow students in the schools and continue to interact with these
students via email. These visits to the community or brief community
inquiry projects are often required in a course, and are calculated to increase students' knowledge of both the community and course topics. The
literature reviewed contained many studies that reported a wide range
of courses that use field trips and/or brief community inquiry projects.

Cooper describes activities used to introduce Teaching Fellows in their junior year seminar to the diverse communities such as "walking a mile in another's shoes," "camera safari," and "debunking the community."[16] In the "walking a mile in another's shoes" activity, for example, students are involved in experiences in which community members might engage such as using public transportation, applying for an hourly wage job, applying for subsidized housing, and eating at a homeless shelter. Cooper reports multiple opportunities for classroom discussions and reflection including field notes, free writes, and interviews. The initial student resistance to going into the community lessen with more exposure, and students start to view diverse communities through "a lens of strengths instead of one filled with deficits" (p. 253). Hyland and Noffke[17] describe community and social inquiry assignments that require their students in a social studies methods course to "cross cultural boundaries to learn about historically marginalized people" from members of those communities (p. 371). In addition to spending two days each week in a classroom, preservice teachers are expected to learn about the neighborhood from which their students come by mapping the resources and services in the neighborhood, talking to community residents, and developing a relationship with a community member. Preservice teachers are encouraged to choose further assignments from a list, which includes such activities as attending religious or cultural events, conducting an oral history, analyzing media documents for cultural representations or omissions, and visiting service organizations that serve particular populations (shelters, food banks, etc.). Preservice teachers process their experience through written reflections and bring videos, performance, pictures, and guest speakers to share their learning with peers.

The emphasis on field trips and brief community inquiry projects is to increase preservice teachers' learning about course topics and diverse contexts. Ultimately, the goal is to enhance student outcomes; that is, their personal, cognitive, and social development. Faculty organizing these opportunities view community engagement as a means for facilitating these goals but many of them report mixed findings about the usefulness of field trip visits and brief community inquiries. For instance, some studies indicate that as evidence of their social development students develop a new understanding of diversity, especially because of the emphasis placed on reflection and classroom-based discussion, while others report reification of deficit-oriented stereotypes about the "other" and their communities. Critics of this category caution that field trips and brief inquiry into diverse communities must be carefully handled as not to reinforce stereotypes or reduce diverse communities into objects of curiosity and study.

Cultural Immersion

The focus in immersion experiences is to deepen preservice teachers' understanding of communities and to cultivate a positive attitude toward cultural diversity. They come to a deeper knowledge about diverse communities as a result of living or interacting with them over one semester or longer. Immersion experiences can be stand-alone or combined with methods courses or the student teaching practicum. They can be organized through schools or directly with communities. Klug and Hall[18] describe an experience in which preservice students from the language arts course completed a practicum of thirty hours at an elementary school serving predominantly American Indian children coupled with substantial interaction with community members. As a result of a university-school-community partnership, preservice teachers, inservice teachers, and community members learned the Shoshoni language in a class that was taught by community members who were native speakers. From this immersion experience, preservice teachers learned about culturally responsive literacy for American Indian children. They also produced an alphabet book that they made available for use in the school and the community. The authors note that this immersion project has resulted in increased learning opportunities for the adults and children involved, and it has also "increased respect for the Shoshoni language by non-Natives in communities throughout Idaho" (p. 39).

The often cited Indiana University's American Indian Reservation Project is probably the most elaborate of cultural immersion programs for preservice teachers. In a seventeen-week semester-long experience, preservice teachers are placed in the Navajo Nation reservation schools where they live in the placement school's dormitory and complete their student-teaching while engaging in ongoing substantive community-based activities. Preparation of the immersion experience takes place in the academic year prior to student teaching. According to Stachowski and Frey, "[p]roject participants are required to undergo extensive preparation (including seminars, readings, workshops, and sessions with Navajo consultants) for the cultural values, beliefs, lifestyles, and educational practices in the placement sites for which they have applied."[19] During their student-teaching, preservice teachers are expected to complete a service-learning project off the school grounds, and activities must adhere to the three Rs of service-learning: realistic, reflective, and reciprocal exchange. Preservice teachers in this program report that much of their learning comes from interacting with families and community members.[20]

Studies reviewed also showed instances when teacher education programs organize shorter CFEs directly with communities. Ference and Bell describe an immersion experience for preservice teachers through Explorations in Diverse Cultures, a two- to three-week course offered in May in a sequence of three courses designed to expose the predominantly White prospective teachers to linguistic and cultural diversity.[21] The teacher education program requires all of their graduates to receive an English for Speakers of Other Languages (ESOL) endorsement. Preservive teachers participating in this immersion experience live with immigrant Latino host families for thirteen days and attend family activities including meals, work, shopping, church, sports, and extended family gatherings. They also observe and teach for ten days at a program serving new immigrants from Mexico as well as from Central and South American countries. Prior to this experience, preservice teachers would have completed seventy or more hours of school-based field experience, helping out and teaching in regular classrooms. They also would have completed six ninety-minute seminars with required readings and participated in class discussions around the readings and the community. While in their community immersion sites, preservice teachers keep journals in which they are encouraged to connect their experience to course readings, and attend ongoing reflection seminars. They are expected to turn in a portfolio that should include a personal philosophy for teaching ESOL students, journal entries, artifacts, and a synthesis essay. In discussing the benefits of this short-term immersion experience, the authors note the development of preservice teachers' insight into immigration, culture, and breaking stereotypes and misconceptions.

Seidl and Seidl and Friend describe an immersion experience organized with an African American community that also involves tutoring. Although this two- to three-hour weekly immersion experience is voluntary, students in the teacher education program work for an entire year with members of an African American church in the various programs organized through the church, including after-school tutoring programs.[22] University faculty and community members hold weekly meetings to help the preservice teachers process their experience and connect it to their coursework and assigned readings. Participating preservice teachers complete their master's project through joint inquiry with community members, and they develop bicultural competency and culturally relevant pedagogies. More importantly, this immersion experience allows students to identify community members as assets and interact with community members as peers of equal status rather than objects of curiosity or study, and results in the preservice teachers gaining important understandings of culture, race, and education. It also allows students to render important service to the community in collaboration with community members.

Studies in the community immersion category suggest that, although preservice teachers may engage in service, the main goal of this CFE remains increasing their knowledge of the communities in question. They also identify important features of effective cultural immersion: prior study of the culture; homestays; involvement in community everyday activities; and frequent reflections on culture, race, power, and their relationship to education. Faculty supporting cultural immersion CFEs see community engagement as a vital way to deepen their students' understanding and experience of diverse cultures. A related goal is to cultivate a deeper appreciation of student diversity. This perspective emphasizes cultivating reciprocal relationships with hosting communities. However, the studies on immersion experiences caution of the multiple, layered intricacies relating to organizing them.

Community Service-Learning

The often cited definition offered by Bringle and Hatcher helps to clarify the main features of the typical service-learning experience. They define service learning as "course-based, credit-bearing educational experience in which students (a) participate in an organized service activity that meets identified community needs, and (b) reflect on the service activity in such a way as to gain further understanding of course content, a broader appreciation of the discipline, and an enhanced sense of civic responsibility."[23] Service learning can be optional or required, and in education it involves a wide array of opportunities ranging from assisting in service agencies and programs located on school grounds and in the community, to community advocacy and research projects. Many studies reviewed for this category focused on service-learning that reflected a service-provider orientation, meaning the focus was on learning through service. Service was direct and indirect as opposed to advocacy or research. Lake and Jones[24] articulate the differences in these four approaches by emphasizing the outcomes on community: "*direct* service is when students' service directly affects and involves recipients, person-to-person or face-to-face; *indirect* service is when students' do not provide service to an individual but to the community as a whole; to create awareness of or promote action on an issue of public interest is the nature of *advocacy*; and *research* involves students' finding, gathering, and reporting on information in public interest." Each approach suggests a different orientation toward the community.

Learning through Direct and Indirect Service to the Community

Students engaged in semester-long, credit bearing service learning experiences help out in community agencies such as shelters, food banks, community educational centers, sports organizations, and after school programs. Service activities include tutoring and mentoring, providing training in skill building, writing proposals, organizing fund raising efforts, and evaluating programs. In addition to performing tasks, students may or may not be expected to conduct brief social inquiry projects in the community, such as community assets mapping, oral histories, and interviews with community members to gain their perspectives on issues studied in class. Direct and indirect service experiences can be organized directly with families, community agencies, or through the school.

Dodd and Lilly and Bondy and Davis present examples of cases where service-learning was organized directly with the community organizations. In Dodd and Lilly, preservice teachers in two universities enrolled in either semester-long language arts or curriculum courses identified community sites and volunteered their time on projects such as providing services to the library, homeless shelters, children's homes, hospitals, clinics, and nursing homes.[25] They also helped organize and implement a family involvement program and engaged in literacy activities such as reading aloud for children and the elderly, translating books and other reading materials to Spanish, book drives, organizing children's drama, and oral histories. They kept logs, planning guides, reflections, and narratives to document their experiences. Preservice teachers involved in these projects reported personal and educational benefits, including intrinsic rewards from helping others and making theory-practice connections. Bondy and Davis describe a ten-week Bright Futures tutoring program involving preservice teachers in a Research in Elementary Education course and students in a public housing neighborhood. Tutors meet with students for one hour, twice a week, at a tutoring site within the neighborhood. Tutors were provided with guidelines on how to design effective tutoring activities for their students. Although this CFE experience was connected to the Research in Elementary Education course through classroom discussions, "there was not a formal structure by which tutors were helped to examine their experience in Bright Futures."[26] An interview with nine Bright Futures tutors revealed that, over time, most of them were able to overcome initial relationship problems and demonstrate forms of caring for their students. They were increasingly able to plan lessons that were informed by students' interests and strengths, which contributed to improved relationships with their students. Studies in this category suggest that service-learning opportunities with community organizations can be highly educative when well organized and adequately supported.

The majority of the studies reviewed for the community service-learning category involved CFEs organized through the school. Burant and Kirby describe a combined foundations of education and general methods course that offered classroom-based (three hours a week) field experience and an additional requirement to complete ten hours or more of either school or community-based experience. Most of the school-based activities also had an element of serving the community with activities such as publishing a newsletter, hosting parent-principal coffee talks, assembling and delivering food baskets to families, and providing child care for the PTO meetings and parent English as a second language classes. Students who opted for CFE engaged in neighborhood expeditions and riding the district school buses as well as brief inquiries into the community through community interviews. The researchers reported mixed findings with some preservice teachers having "deepening" and "transformative" experiences that increased their desire to teach in diverse schools. Over half had "masked," "partially miseducative," and "escaping" experiences and retained the desire not to teach in diverse settings.[27]

Wiggins et al. present another example of service-learning organized through the school. The study focuses on a group of preservice teachers involved in a year-long school-based practicum that also allowed them the opportunity to work closely with an agency that ran a tutoring program and offered weekly parent education classes. Preservice teachers "worked with tutors and were required to assist with the parent education classes periodically throughout the year."[28] Studies with similar emphases describe preservice teachers involved with organizing activities that brought parents into the school to participate in activities such as family math night and family literacy night. School-based service-learning is often well supported by the school structures but it can also have serious limitations in the sense that it reflects the schools' conceptions of the needs in community.

Another well-represented type of service-learning connected to the school focuses on preservice teachers organizing volunteer community service or service-learning opportunities for K–12 students in their placement schools. Usually preservice teachers are in practica connected to methods of teaching courses or student teaching. Teacher educators seek to place preservice teachers with host teachers who are themselves utilizing service-learning pedagogy with their K–12 students. Baldwin et al. report on preservice teachers who involved fourth and sixth grade students in an oral history project through Partners in Learning (PAL), a four-week summer tutoring and/or mentoring requirement for the undergraduate content literacy course organized in collaboration with fourth and sixth grade teachers. Through the oral history project students received direct guidance in researching and writing about their community over six meetings of about seventy-five minutes each. Preservice teachers kept a portfolio that included lesson plans, in-depth reflections for each lesson, and a final reflection paper. Through this CFE, preservice teachers overcame preconceived notions about diverse learners, although there were instances when negative assumptions were reinforced. The researchers reported that, overall, this service-learning positively affected "preservice teachers' dispositions toward teaching in diverse settings."[29]

Lake and Jones report a two-day-a-week, semester-long practicum offered to preservice teachers enrolled in an Early Childhood Curriculum and Methods course. Preservice teachers designed and implemented service-learning projects involving K and first grade students in projects around gardening, pollution, recycling, environmental awareness, letter-writing, food drives, and hurricane relief efforts. Preservice teachers wrote thematic teaching units and service learning plans. The researchers noted that the use of service-learning projects provided preservice teachers with meaningful learning opportunities and affirmed in teacher educators the usefulness of service-learning as an "avenue for teaching in an integrated or constructivist manner."[30] The findings of this study support a commonly expressed argument that to encourage preservice teachers to use service-learning with their future K–12 students, they should receive explicit instruction and relevant experience with teachers who are skilled in the service-learning pedagogy.[31]

The category of CFEs involving learning through direct and indirect service was well represented in the literature reviewed for this chapter. As mentioned earlier, in this category, CFEs seem to espouse the service provider perspective on community engagement, and the preservice teachers play the role of "knowledge broker or service provider."[32] In this role, they gain personal and academic benefits and increase their interest for teaching in diverse settings. Diverse communities and individuals also benefit from the tasks performed by the preservice teachers. However, the service provider orientation may perpetuate a split between providers and recipients that is often false and inhibit deep explorations or under-standings of issues facing "serviced" families or communities.[33] This split is especially likely to occur when partnering with schools, programs, or agencies that are run by people who are not members of the target minority communities. Because direct and indirect CFEs are the most commonly used in education, the challenge for education faculty is to design experiences that move preservice teachers from merely performing tasks in agencies or programs to a deeper engagement with communities, challenging them to actively investigate the needs of the community and develop projects that would best match those needs. Projects developed should be steeped in an orientation that supports a complex understanding of and participation in the target communities. Community research and/or advocacy focused CFEs provide one example of how this orientation may be cultivated.

Learning through Community Research or Advocacy

In the literature reviewed for this chapter, studies involving community-based research and/or advocacy were few compared than those involving direct and indirect service. Preservice teachers involved in research and/or advocacy-based CFEs are expected to grapple with a problem or challenge facing the community and develop solutions. They can either do this as a class, or collaboratively with community members. Preservice teachers either possess or are trained in specific skills that will allow them to collaborate as trainers, research assistants, program designers or evaluators, grant writers, or media advertising of events/fairs/campaigns. They use these skills to advocate for the community creating awareness or promoting action on an issue facing the community. Advocacy may or may not involve community-based research. While engaged in community-based research or advocacy, students' roles shift between learners, teachers, and collaborators with the community. Boyle-Baise describes the Banneker History Project (BHP) in which twenty-four preservice teachers participating in an honors seminar were involved in a two-year effort to research the history of the Banneker School which existed in the current location of the Banneker Community Center. The BHP was a community initiative that "sought to reconstruct the history of a segregated local school" as a way to build community, affirm diversity, and address inequality in the community.[34] Students spent about fifteen hours in the field, and wrote reflective essays in which they considered their learning about course topics organized around "culturally responsive teaching, funds of knowledge, and asset-based community development." They participated in collections of oral history, conducted interviews with past directors, and created biographies alongside high school and elementary school participants. Preservice teachers also hosted public events such as panels and presentations of their research. They reported developing a deeper understanding of culturally responsive pedagogy and an appreciation of "local adults as funds of historical knowledge." The BHP seemed to "jump-start an asset-based, culturally-sensitive, justice-oriented view of communities."[35]

Cuban and Anderson describe a course entitled Service Leadership for Social Justice offered to preservice teachers, in which, in addition to course readings on social justice issues in education, preservice teachers engaged in thirty-five hours of service-learning in classrooms and community agencies. Their engagement was organized around action research, and the community outcomes of their projects included "increasing city funding for human services, obtaining housing for migrant workers, and advocating for stores to move into poor neighborhoods." Although this study is scanty on the details of how this research was conducted, and the role, if any, that was played by the community members in this process, the authors observed that "preservice teachers continued to use service-learning from a social justice perspective in their school classrooms after their university course." Other outcomes for preservice teachers included increasing levels of critical thinking and cultural competence and developing a stronger service ethic. Cuban and Anderson caution, from their analysis of this and similar case studies, that service-learning from a social justice perspective involves the recognition and constant minding of "fragile boundaries" between the campus and the community.[36]

As mentioned earlier, compared to the literature on other forms of service-learning experiences, studies addressing the research/advocacy category were hard to find in the literature reviewed. However, in the few available, faculty perspective suggests that community engagement involves participation in and with community in solving identified community challenges. Effective community research or advocacy CFEs are supported by readings on the target community, training in specific skills, equal-status interactions with community participants, and a constant reflection on action. CFEs in this category emphasize the need for reciprocity, a focus on students *and* community outcomes, along with a focus on social justice. They usually involve defined projects that are carried out collaboratively with community members. Researchers caution that such projects require a creative use of time, a highly collaborative campus-community relationship, as well a forthright discussion about the "worth of community service to teacher preparation."[37]

THE IMPORTANCE OF FACULTY PERSPECTIVE IN CFES

One of the questions guiding this chapter asked how teacher education programs amid the array of competing demands infuse in their curriculum field experiences that focus on diverse communities. The studies reviewed for this chapter provide us with the "what," that is, examples of the opportunities teacher educators provide for preservice teachers to interact with diverse communities in their education as future teachers. Teacher educators provide these opportunities in three broad categories: field trips and brief community inquiry projects; immersion; and service-learning. Although it is accurate to say that these categories differ in key aspects, these differences may not be so clear cut as to help answer a more urgent question for teacher educators considering using CFEs for the first time: Which CFEs are most appropriate for educating teachers for diversity? This is a harder question to answer. The temptation for teacher educators seeking to use CFEs is to focus on such immediate concerns as the length of time, types of reflection, and nature of activities for their students while in the field. Such a focus, while useful, may not provide the clarity needed to design useful CFEs. This is mainly because the three categories mentioned above are not mutually exclusive, and there are many examples from the studies reviewed where there are similarities across categories in these aspects. What may be useful for such educators is to first articulate clearly their perspectives on community engagement and use this understanding to design CFEs that reflect these perspectives. Although only a few of the studies reviewed for this chapter articulated the instructors' perspectives on community engagement, four broad understandings of the importance of community engagement in preservice teacher education are evident. They are community engagement as a way to: facilitate academic engagement with course materials focused on diversity; develop an awareness of the cultures of America's diverse populations; cultivate an ethic of service toward people in need; and participate in community efforts for social change.

In first clarifying their perspectives toward community engagement, educators may avoid choosing CFEs that may undermine their goals for their students. For example, educators who emphasize brief visits to diverse communities unfamiliar to their students for the purpose of facilitating engagement with course topics risk developing in their students an insufficient knowledge and a reification of previously held stereotypes. Some educators have argued that this harm can be mitigated by building in the course relevant readings on culture, race, power, and opportunities for discussion and reflection. Similarly, teacher educators who emphasize cultural immersion can help preservice teachers learn to identify community assets, acquire deep appreciation of cultures unfamiliar to them, and develop cross-cultural communication and other skills needed for teaching diverse students. Whether immersion experiences are short or long, some strategies seem to facilitate the attainment of these goals: prior study of the target culture; "equal-status" interaction with community members; participation in everyday life in the community; and frequent reflection on experience in the context of relevant readings. The goals of educators who embrace service-learning may differ depending on whether they see community engagement merely as a service to the less fortunate or an opportunity to effect social change in collaboration with those that are affected by social problems. Clarifying the educator's perspective with regard to community engagement is important for individual educators in determining the type of CFEs that best serves their pedagogical goals.

INSTITUTIONALIZING CFES IN TEACHER EDUCATION

This section address the second question guiding this chapter: How can CFEs be institutionalized in teacher education programs? In addressing this question I draw on Hartley, Harkavy, and Benson's observation that suggests that for the institutionalization of CFEs to occur, CFEs need to be pervasive, supported by adequate structures, and express core values of the department. I argue that three broad understandings should inform any efforts toward institutionalization. The understandings are that CFEs should: be situated at the department level and infused throughout the teacher education curriculum; be supported by departmental structures; and be situated within a broader vision of teacher education that is community-engaged. The premise here is that CFEs are an important curricular component of programs committed to educating teachers for diversity, and thus should be fully embedded in these programs. In chapter 1, the notion of community-engaged teacher education was introduced and defined as a concept and practice that allows curricular and structural changes that support educating teachers for diversity through community engagement. Engaged programs should see the institutionalization of CFEs as vital to their existence.

Engaged programs should seek to not just infuse CFEs in education courses, but do so in ways that suggest department ownership of the process. Department ownership of CFEs is important because just infusing CFEs in single courses without integrating them throughout the teacher education curriculum does not lead to enduring changes. The bulk of studies considered for this chapter tended to describe CFEs within the context of one course, without necessarily contextualizing the discussion within the broader teacher education program. This stand-alone course model for infusing CFEs, while most common in teacher education programs, is too haphazard and fragmented to enable the kind of coherence needed to prepare teachers for diversity. Although the literature review for this chapter did not provide studies that showed the depth of integration suggested here, there were a few examples of two-course integration that are instructive. Buck and Sylvester, for example, organized a CFE aimed at helping preservice teachers question their perceptions of an inner-city neighborhood and to identify structural issues affecting the urban communities. The CFE was offered in the context of a foundations course (School and Society) and a social studies methods course, and resulted in increased collaboration among faculty and deepened understanding of research and curriculum development around neighborhood studies among students.[38] Burant and Kirby report a similar integration of a Foundations of Education course and a general method course that helped foster collaboration among faculty, transforming their pedagogy and deepening students' knowledge of the surrounding community. The goal of curricular integration is to situate CFEs at the departmental level and infuse them throughout the entire teacher education curriculum. Conceptualizing CFEs as a departmental concern, rather than an individual instructor's, can not only reduce the fragmentation that is typical in the stand-alone course model but also help articulate clearly the scope and sequence of CFEs and ways they can be infused in the entire program in more deliberate ways. Such coherence also serves to deepen both the disciplinary knowledge and knowledge about teaching diverse students. CFEs should provide multiple opportunities to reflect on community experiences and linking them to academic content. Faculty collaboration is essential to organizing this knowledge base. Buck and Sylvester and Burant and Kirby mentioned above are good examples of how faculty collaboration led to an integrated view of CFEs across two courses, allowing them to experiment with formats that fostered collegiality, deepened students' knowledge about issues facing diverse populations, and led to more program-based conversations about CFEs. An integrated approach also ensures that students are not subjected to too much CFEs in their course-work, as this might cause "community fatigue" and/or breed resentment. A careful sequencing of CFEs helps in organizing the knowledge base in ways that facilitate student learning.

A second understanding that can support the institutionalization of CFEs is that CFEs should be supported by departmental structures to ensure their integration throughout the teacher education curriculum. The goal is to accommodate CFEs from early on in the preparation process, allowing for more than one short interaction with communities. Darling-Hammond reports on Wheelock College's teacher education curriculum where courses place first-year prospective teachers in nonschool settings, such as community centers, after-school programs, and Big Sister programs. A director of field placement is charged with the responsibility of "selecting settings that address the student teacher's needs and stretch his or her experience base, challenge preconceptions, and expand understanding of children, families, and communities."[39] CFEs continue throughout the preparation process. Having multiple or prolonged, rather than short-term single, CFEs in low-income and linguistically and culturally diverse communities is likely to improve the learning experiences of the preservice teachers. Personnel can help enhance coherence and sequencing needed to support student learning. A CFE coordinator can ensure that students are prepared to have access to engage in diverse, sequenced, and complex experiences that build on prior experiences. They can also serve to develop sustained reciprocal relationships between teacher education programs and diverse communities, allowing for a steady flow of students and faculty into communities throughout the year, somewhat mitigating some of the deleterious effects on communities associated with short-term field experiences and research. In the absence of additional personnel, departments can form links with campus-wide structures and personnel involved with coordinating community-based learning initiatives to fulfill some of these functions.

A third understanding is that CFEs should operate within a broader program vision that is community-engaged, one that is committed to addressing disparities in K–12 education, values diversity, and acknowledges the important role that diverse communities can play in teacher education. A shared program vision for educating teachers for diversity through community engagement is critical. In chapter 1, I stressed that such a vision can be enhanced when programs among other things

- have a commitment to address educational disparities in K–12 education
- embrace community-based pedagogy and infuse CFEs in the curriculum
- actively recruit, retain, and support faculty committed to community engagement
- recruit preservice teachers committed to teaching in diverse settings
- develop collaborative and reciprocal relationships with diverse communities
- espouse the role of the teacher as a social change agent

When taken together, the three broad understandings outlined above—that CFEs should be situated at the department level and infused throughout the teacher education curriculum; that CFEs need to be supported by departmental structures, including curricular and personnel; and that CFEs should be situated within a broader vision of teacher education that is community-engaged—can help support the institutionalization of CFEs in community-engaged teacher education programs.

CONCLUSION

CFEs are increasingly viewed as critical to the process of educating teachers for diversity. A review of studies from teacher education literature reveals three broad categories of CFEs in use in education, and all three categories may differ in terms of degree of integration in education courses, time commitment, nature of student activities, types of structured reflection, and curricular benefits. I emphasize that teacher educators wishing to use CFEs in their practice should foremost clarify their perspective about community engagement and use this understanding to design appropriate CFEs. Similarly, teacher education programs committed to educating teachers for diversity should seek to institutionalize CFEs. The institutionalization of CFEs suggests, in the words of Seidl and Friend, "changing our habits"[40] with regard to educating teachers for diversity. This involves developing department-coordinated infusion in education courses, structural supports, and a shared vision to guide the two. Discussions regarding how to institutionalize CFEs are important because in their absence CFEs may continue to receive the cursory and fragmented treatment that prevails in traditional teacher education programs. Such treatment may lead to a superficial and sometimes harmful conception of community engagement and its role in teacher education.

NOTES

1. See Ronald Ferguson, *Toward Excellence with Equity: An Emerging Vision for Closing the Achievement Gap* (Cambridge, MA: Harvard Education Press, 2007); Carol Deshano da Silva, James Huguley, Zenub Kakli, and Radhika Rao, eds., *The Opportunity Gap: Achievement and Inequality in Education* (Cambridge, MA: Harvard Education Press, 2007); Gary Orfield, *Dropouts in America: Confronting the Graduation Rate Crisis* (Cambridge, MA: Harvard Education Press, 2004; Norma Gonzáles, Luis C. Moll, and Cathy Amanti, eds., *Funds of Knowledge: Theorizing Practices in Households, Communities, and Classroom* (Mahwah, NJ: L. Erlbaum Associates, 2005); Joyce Epstein, *School, Family, and Community Partnerships: Preparing Educators and Improving Schools* (Boulder, CO: Westview Press, 2001).

2. "Knowledge base" is a concept that was popularized by Lee Shulman. See Lee Shulman, "Knowledge and Teaching: Foundations of the New Reform," *Harvard Educational Review* (February 1987): 1–22.

3. National Council for Accreditation of Teacher Education (NCATE), "Professional Standards for the Accreditation of Teacher Preparation Institutions," 2008, http://www.ncate.org/documents/standards/NCATE%20Standards%202008 .pdf (accessed September 18, 2008).

4. Carl A. Grant and Maureen Gillette, "A Candid Talk to Teacher Educators about Effectively Preparing Teachers Who Can Teach Everyone's Children," *Journal of Teacher Education* 57, no. 3 (May/June 2006): 292–99.

5. Quoted in Margaret Gallego, "Is Experience the Best Teacher? The Potential of Coupling Classroom and Community-Based Field Experiences," *Journal of Teacher Education* 52, no. 4 (2001): 312–25.

6. Mari Koerner and Najwa Abdul-Tawwab, "Using Community as a Resource for Teacher Education: A Case Study," *Equity & Excellence in Education* 39 (2006): 37–46.

7. Carol Myers and Terry Pickeral, "Service-Learning: An Essential Process for Preparing Teachers as Transformational Leaders in the Reform of Public Education," in *Learning with the Community: Concepts and Models for Service Learning in*

Teacher Education, ed. Joseph Erickson and Jeffrey Anderson (Sterling, VA: Stylus Publishing, LLC, 2005), 13.

8. Community engagement perspective in CFE is being used here to refer to a focus on cultivating deep understandings of and reciprocal relationships with diverse contexts for the purpose of educating teachers for diversity.

9. Jeffrey B. Anderson and Joseph A. Erickson, "Service-Learning in Preservice Teacher Education," *Academic Exchange Quarterly* (Summer 2003): 111–15.

10. Quoted in Sondra Cuban and Jeffrey B. Anderson, "Where's the Justice in Service-Learning? Institutionalizing Service-Learning from a Social Justice Perspective at a Jesuit University," *Equity & Excellence in Education* 40, no. 2 (2007): 144–155; Education Commission of the States (ECS), "Learning That Lasts: How Service-Learning Can Become an Integral Part of Schools, States and Communities," 2002, http://www.ecs.org/clearinghouse/40/54/4054.pdf (accessed February 26, 2010).

11. Matthew Hartley, Ira Harkavy, and Lee Benson, "Putting Down Roots in the Groves of Academe: The Challenges of Institutionalizing Service-Learning," in *Service-Learning in Higher Education: Critical Issues and Directions*, ed. Dan W. Butin (New York: Palgrave Macmillan, 2005), 205–22.

12. Etta Hollins and Maria Torres Guzman, "Research on Preparing Teachers for Diverse Populations," in *Studying Teacher Education: The Report of the AERA Panel on Research and Teacher Education*, ed. Marilyn Cochran-Smith and Kenneth M. Zeichner (Mahwah, NJ: Lawrence Erlbaum Associates, 2005), 477–548.

13. See Ken Zeichner, Susan Melnick, and Mary Louise Gomez, eds., *Currents of Reform in Preservice Teacher Education* (New York: Teachers College Press, 1996); Christine Sleeter, "Preparing White Teachers for Diverse Students," in *Handbook of Research on Teacher Education: Enduring Questions in Changing Contexts*, ed. Marilyn Cochran-Smith, Sharon Feiman-Nemser, D. John McIntyre, and Kelly Demers (New York: Routledge and Association of Teacher Educators, 2008), 551–58 ; Etta Hollins and Maria Torres Guzman, "Research on Preparing Teachers," 477.

14. See Marilynne Boyle-Baise and D. John McIntyre, "What Kind of Experience? Preparing Teachers in PDS or Community Settings," in *Handbook of Research on Teacher Education*, 307–30; Peter Murrell, *The Community Teacher: A New Framework for Effective Urban Teaching* (New York: Teachers College Press, 2001).

15. See Robert A. Wiggins, Eric J. Follo, and Mary B. Eberly, "The Impact of a Field Immersion Program on Pre-Service Teachers' Attitudes toward Teaching in Culturally Diverse Classrooms," *Teaching and Teacher Education* 23, no. 5 (2007): 653–63; Terry J. Burant and Dan Kirby, "Beyond Classroom-Based Early Field Experiences: Understanding an Educative Practicum in an Urban School and Community," *Teaching and Teacher Education* 18 (2002): 561–75.

16. Jewell E. Cooper, "Strengthening the Case for Community-Based Learning in Teacher Education," *Journal of Teacher Education* 58, no. 3 (2007): 245–55.

17. Nora E. Hyland and Susan E. Noffke, "Understanding Diversity through Social and Community Inquiry: An Action-Research Study," *Journal of Teacher Education*, 56 (September/October 2005): 367–81.

18. Beverly J. Klug and Janice Hall, "Opening Doors to Wisdom: Working Together for Our Children," *Action in Teacher Education* 24, no. 2 (Summer 2002): 34–41.

19. Laura L. Stachowski and Christopher J. Frey, "Lessons Learned in Navajoland: Student Teachers Reflect on Professional and Cultural Learning in Reservation Schools and Communities," *Action in Teacher Education* 25, no. 3 (2003): 38–47.

20. See also Laura Stachowski and James M. Mahan, "Cross-Cultural Field Placements: Student Teachers Learning from Schools and Communities," *Theory Into Practice* 37, no. 2 (1998): 154–62; Laura Stachowski, Jayson Richardson, and Michelle Henderson, "Student Teachers Report on the Influence of Cultural Values on Classroom Practice and Community Involvement: Perspectives from the Navajo Reservation and from Abroad," *Teacher Educator* 39, no. 1 (2003): 52–63.

21. Ruth A. Ference and Steven Bell, "A Cross-Cultural Immersion in the U.S.: Changing Preservice Teacher Attitudes toward Latino ESOL Students," *Equity & Excellence in Education* 37, no. 4 (2004): 343–50.

22. Barbara Seidl, "Working with Communities to Explore and Personalize Culturally Relevant Pedagogies: Push, Double Images, and Raced Talk," *Journal of Teacher Education* 58, no. 2 (2007): 168–83; Barbara Seidl and Gloria Friend, "Unification of Church and State: Universities and Churches Working Together to Nurture Anti-racist, Biculturally Competent Teachers," *Journal of Teacher Education* 53, no. 2 (2002): 142–52; "Leaving Authority at the Door: Equal Status Community-Based Experiences and the Preparation of Teachers for Diverse Classrooms," *Teaching and Teacher Education* 18, no. 4 (2002b): 421–33.

23. Robert G. Bringle and Julie Hatcher, "Institutionalization of Service Learning in Higher Education," *Journal of Higher Education* 17, no. 3 (2000): 27–90.

24. Vickie E. Lake and Ithel Jones, "Service-Learning in Early Childhood Teacher Education: Using Service to Put Meaning Back into Learning Teaching and Teacher Education," *Teaching and Teacher Education* 24, no. 8 (November 2008): 2148.

25. Elizabeth L. Dodd and Dana H. Lilly, "Learning within Communities: An Investigation of Community Service-Learning in Teacher Education," *Action in Teacher Education* 22, no. 3 (Fall 2000): 77–85.

26. Elizabeth Bondy and Steven Davis, "The Caring of Strangers: Insights from a Field Experience in a Culturally Unfamiliar Community," *Action in Teacher Education* 22, no. 2 (Summer 2000): 54–66.

27. Terry J. Burant and Dan Kirby, "Beyond Classroom-Based Early Field Experiences," 565–71.

28. Robert A. Wiggins, Eric J. Follo, and Mary B. Eberly, "The Impact of a Field Immersion," 656.

29. Shelia C. Baldwin, Alice M. Buchanan, and Mary E. Rudisill, "What Teacher Candidates Learned About Diversity, Social Justice, and Themselves from Service-Learning Experiences," *Journal of Teacher Education* 58, no. 4 (2007): 315–27.

30. Vickie E. Lake and Ithel Jones, "Service-Learning in Early Childhood Teacher Education," 2153.

31. See Joseph Erickson and Jeffrey Anderson, eds., *Learning with the Community*.

32. Etta Hollins and Maria Torres Guzman, "Research on Preparing Teachers for Diverse Populations," 493.

33. See David Donahue, Jane Boyer, and Dana Rosenberg, "Learning with and Learning From: Reciprocity in Service Learning in Teacher Education," *Equity & Excellence in Education* 36, no. 1 (2003): 15–17.

34. Marilynne Boyle-Baise, "Preparing Community-Oriented Teachers: Reflections from a Multicultural Service-Learning Project," *Journal of Teacher Education* 56, no. 5 (2005): 447–58.

35. Marilynne Boyle-Baise, "Preparing Community-Oriented Teachers," 447–56.

36. Sondra Cuban and Jeffrey B. Anderson, "Where's the Justice in Service-Learning?" 150–52.

37. Marilynne Boyle-Baise, "Preparing Community-Oriented Teachers," 456.

38. Patricia Buck and Paul Skilton Sylvester, "Preservice Teachers Enter Urban Communities: Coupling Funds of Knowledge Research and Critical Pedagogy in Teacher Education," in *Funds of Knowledge: Theorizing Practices in Households, Communities, and Classrooms*, ed. Norma Gonzáles, Luis C. Moll, and Cathy Amanti (Mahwah, NJ: Lawrence Erlbaum Associates, Publishers, 2005), 213–32.

39. Linda Darling-Hammond, *Powerful Teacher Education* (San Francisco, CA: Jossey-Bass, 2005), 229.

40. Barbara Seidl and Gloria Friend, "The Unification of Church and State."

3

❧

Can the Village Educate the Prospective Teacher? Reflections on Multicultural Service-Learning in African American Communities[1]

As noted in chapter 1, service-learning, as a way of connecting academic learning and relevant community service, has gained prominence in the American higher education landscape since the 1980s. In many departments of education, however, "community" has come to mean mainly K–12 schools within the immediate vicinity of the university or college. Teacher educators in these institutions of higher learning form partnerships with K–12 schools that provide opportunities for service-learning and internship experiences for their students. The professional development school model has been particularly successful at establishing university–school partnerships and involving higher education faculty and students in the education of K–12 students.[2] Few educators, however, have reached out to diverse communities for similar partnerships, despite a growing body of literature suggesting that college students accrue academic benefits as well as a self-awareness of values such as multiculturalism, civic responsibility, and social justice from engaging in community-based organizations (CBOs) with ethnic and racial minorities. Acknowledging that this challenge exists, some teacher educators are urging their colleagues to involve preservice teachers in what is now known as multicultural service-learning (MSL).[3] MSL, they argue, can provide a means to engage especially preservice teachers preparing to teach African American students in communities through CBOs.

This chapter supports the call to engage preservice teachers in CBOs serving African American communities, specifically the education oriented community-based programs (CBPs). I argue that CBPs serving African

American children are more than responses to perceived shortcomings in the mainstream school system. They also function as alternative sites for educational activity and promising sites for teachers preparing to teach African American students. Education here is understood as defined by Murrell as "a total process of promoting the intellectual, spiritual, ethical, and social development of young people . . . stewarding them into capable, caring, and character-rich adulthood."[4] CBPs in African American communities exist in a variety of formal and informal, voluntary, and non-profit groups and organizations that engage in several activities in various settings. These can include religious institutions, after-school programs, grassroots organizations, community centers, local libraries, social clubs, sports clubs, and local chapters of national groups (e.g., Boys and Girls Clubs). Some popular CBPs offered within these structures include Saturday schools, a variety of literacy programs, the rites of passage programs or African American male- or female-oriented programs, and homework and tutoring programs, some operated in partnerships with schools.

The chapter also emphasizes that CBPs are important educational sites that have not been optimally used by teacher educators for teacher preparation and community engagement. If this claim is to be taken seriously, we must ask several related questions. Why is there such little interest among teacher educators to reach out to African American CBPs as sites for community engagement and preparation of future teachers? Why should teacher educators pay attention to CBPs among African American communities? What are the possibilities and challenges involved in using African American communities as sites for community engagement and teacher preparation? How can campus–community relationships involving African American CBPs be strengthened? Answers to these questions are important because they suggest that learning about African American children and effective pedagogy for them can be enhanced if teacher education programs strengthen partnerships with African American communities. In this chapter, I reflect on these questions and review a cross section of literature on the role of CBPs in the education of African American children and youth. I also reflect on multicultural service-learning in African American CBPs, and share insights drawn from my experience as faculty in education involving students in MSL. I stress that MSL is an important element of a community-engaged teacher education.

COMMUNITY-BASED PROGRAMS AS
ALTERNATIVE SITES FOR EDUCATIONAL ACTIVITY

In this section, I examine the notion of CBPs in African American communities and present examples. In many African American communities, CBPs are located within CBOs, which act as bridges between the home and service-providing institutions such as the school. In African American communities facing challenges such as poverty, urban violence, drugs, dysfunctional homes, and so on, CBOs are critical in supporting the growth and development of young people[5] and often provide "resources that extend beyond family and schools."[6] CBOs also serve as purveyors of African American culture and sites for community building.[7] More importantly, they serve as sites where students can experience deeply educational activities in culturally affirming contexts, with the goal of individual and community empowerment. Ball summed up the multifaceted function of CBOs in African American communities:

> Historically, community-based organizations have served as social, cultural, and political spaces in which African Americans have been able to assert their right and their responsibility not only to read, write, and understand, but also to gain new literacy skills needed for them to transform their life experiences. Community-based organizations have also served as spaces where African Americans have been able to contribute their voices to wider projects of possibility and community empowerment.[8]

Like CBOs, CBPs play a variety of roles which make them one of the most influential factors in the education of many African Americans.[9] In highlighting the educational role played by CBPs, it is important to examine some of the educational activities that take place in literacy programs, Saturday school, and other programs mentioned previously. Literature on the subject reveals three unique features, which evoke the popular African adage, "It takes a village to raise a child," and tend to characterize these programs: (1) a holistic view of the learner that advocates a pursuit of intellectual development while also paying attention to social, affective, moral, and political dimensions of development of children and youth; (2) the understanding that race and identity play a significant role in the education of African American children and youth. In other words, race continues to matter in education just as it does in society at large and, as a result, it can be argued that educators of, and educational programs for, African American students must see color in order to be effective; and (3) a pedagogy grounded in culturally responsive practices or what Boykin et al. called the "Afro-cultural ethos,"[10] one that is historically and racially grounded. As the following examples show, these three areas of emphasis are likely to be present in varying degrees in many CBPs serving African American students.

Ball and Lardner discuss three CBPs serving African American communities.[11] One specific example is relevant here. The program called Ujima (a Swahili word meaning "collective work and responsibility") meets on two to three Saturdays each month in a church to provide urban African

American girls, ages six to eighteen, with language, literacy, and life skills learning activities. The program, with an average weekly attendance of sixty to seventy-five girls, uses the rites of passage model in which African American adult instructors engage the participating youth in several learning activities, including impromptu oral performances, memorized recitations, reading, writing, literature, drama, art, music, dance, and so forth. According to Ball and Lardner, CBPs like Ujima provide African American youth with numerous opportunities to access "adult role models that support them with opportunities to experiment with language and literacy interaction models that not only reflect standards of the dominant society but also standards of the students' cultures."[12] A deeper look at the philosophy, goals, and activities of the Ujima program shows clearly how it reflects the three characteristics of African American CBPs outlined above.

Warfield-Coppock provided further examples of the rites of passage CBPs in African American communities.[13] These programs probably present the best example of instruction for social, affective, and moral development steeped in cultural relevance and empowerment at both individual and community levels. Rites of passage programs are based on traditional African systems of socialization through which youth are mentored into adult roles and responsibilities. These programs can be school and/or community based. Harvey wrote of an after-school manhood development program in Washington, DC, in which "[t]he emphasis is on youths interacting with youths to develop constructive lifestyles and positive solutions to life problems, as well as to recognize their personal and cultural strengths and abilities."[14] In these programs, participating youth are provided with a structure that values and respects them while demanding that they step up to their roles as productive members of the community. These programs are likely to appeal to African American youth who do not always feel validated or valued in a racist system.

The legendary Algebra Project remains an enduring illustration of both the intellectual development emphasis and connectedness to community building and empowerment elements. The project "was born out of one parent's concern with the mathematics education of his children," but "first took root in Boston at Freedom House, a community-based organization."[15] Bob Moses, the founder of the Algebra Project, "considers higher math to be key to economic equality."[16] The acclaim for the Algebra Project among African American communities is in no small part due to its grassroots nature and its goal of empowering African American students to be successful in mathematics, and hence all schooling. Math success and school success are almost synonymous because of the gatekeeping role that math, especially algebra, is understood to play in the school system. Academic success is of course considered a means of social and economic advancement in many African American communities.

Many CBPs in the African American communities are like the Algebra Project in the sense that they are sparked by the vision of an individual or a group committed to the intellectual, social, economic, and political empowerment of African Americans. The Books of Hope project in Somerville, Massachusetts, is another good example of a community-based literacy program with humble beginnings.

> In March 1999, Anika Nailah, [an African American] writer . . . walked over to the Mystic Housing Development in Somerville, and proposed an idea. She believed in the passionate intelligence of young people . . . she wanted to work with them to liberate the hopes that lived in their hearts . . . she believed that she could help the youth in Mystic write, publish, and sell their own books.[17]

Doug Holder, reporting on an interview with Nailah, observes that, since 1999, "the program has trained kids from the projects and elsewhere in four key areas: writing, publishing, performing, marketing and outreach. The youth are involved in many aspects of producing a book, and their development is advanced through a writer-in-residence, guest artists and mentors, as well as field trips." The youth, most of whom are of color and come from economically challenged backgrounds, get to keep the proceeds from the sale of their books.[18] Other programs for promoting literacy among African American youth in their communities are detailed in the research by Busch and Ball.[19] They document work that is being done by groups such as Streetside Stories, Youth Speaks, and WritersCorps, which offer literacy instruction to youth in culturally affirming contexts within their communities. Busch and Ball's investigation of community-based writing programs reveals that these programs use culturally responsive pedagogical approaches to help young people become effective, enthusiastic writers within their communities.

A final example that I am familiar with as a participant-observer is the Academic and other Initiatives for Maximum Success program that meets on Saturday in the college town of Amherst, Massachusetts. The program supports academic and cultural awareness, as well as personal and community-building goals for Black students attending the local public schools. Founded in 2004 by a grassroots parent group concerned with the academic success of African American children and youth in Amherst public schools, the program uses community- and college-based volunteers to provide academic support. The program also engages participants in culturally enriching activities, including lectures, sports and games, movie discussions, field trips, and potluck socials. This wide range of activities reflects the three-pronged focus of the program: providing instruction to African American children to enhance their academic success, especially in math, literacy, and science; using the human and material resources residing in the African American communities to build culturally affirming contexts to support the holistic education of these children and youth; and drawing on the image of the village, providing a culturally affirming and supportive community for them through family and community-building social activities. Since its inception, the organization has seen increased participation by families and students in its activities, and appears to have taken root in the Black community in Amherst.[20]

The preceding discussion demonstrates that CBPs in African American communities serve as more than just alternative sites for educational activity. The distinguishing element of many African American CBPs, compared to mainstream programs, is their vision of what a good education for African American students might entail. It is also significant to note that in many cases key individuals involved in CBPs are well-educated persons of color who have made deliberate efforts to connect their work in institutions of higher learning with civic engagement work. Evans[21] speaks to this distinguishing characteristic and its long history among African American educators. I now turn to a central question posed earlier in this chapter: Why should teacher educators pay attention to CBPs among African American communities?

CULTURALLY RESPONSIVE EDUCATION FOR PRESERVICE TEACHERS PREPARING TO TEACH AFRICAN AMERICAN STUDENTS

The demographic challenge and manifest shortcomings of current teacher education in preparing effective teachers of African American students underscore the need to pay attention to CBPs. The demographic challenge is widely discussed in literature, and is summarized by Cooper when she noted that over 40 percent of school-age children are students of color. "Of these, 17.25 percent of students enrolled in public schools are Black . . . Black teachers represent only 7.3 percent of public school teachers, whereas more than 90 percent are White."[22] It would seem necessary that preservice teachers with limited familiarity and skills to engage with students of color and their communities receive this education in the course of their teacher preparation. The reality in a typical program does not reflect this concern. Often, preservice teachers are likely to be exposed to coursework and a series of field experiences that leave them inadequately prepared to teach students of other racial, ethnic, cultural, and class backgrounds. Examining the gaps in the preparation of teachers of African American students, Ladson-Billings noted:

> With very few exceptions, the literature does not expressly address the preparation of teachers to teach African American learners effectively. . . . Instead, references to the educational needs of African American students are folded into a discourse of deprivation. Searches of the literature base indicate that when one uses the descriptor, "Black education," one is directed to see, "culturally deprived" and "culturally disadvantaged." Thus the educational research literature, when it considers African American learners at all, has constructed all African American children, regardless of economic or social circumstance, within the deficit paradigm.[23]

Few field experiences in teacher education programs explicitly seek to expose preservice teachers to other views of the African American child beyond the deficit perspective that Ladson-Billings refers to here.[24] It may be that many preservice teachers are receiving an education that could potentially harm African American students. I emphasize in this chapter that CBPs in many African American communities may present alternative views of African American students and their communities and potentially counter some of the harmful education to which Ladson-Billings alluded. The available literature suggests that while CBPs undoubtedly serve mainstream education objectives by offering supplementary schooling, they also engender spaces of contestation to the racialized and often deficit notions of African American students and their communities that frame mainstream education thought and practice. This is more often the case for grassroots CBPs. For these reasons and others, education faculty should seriously consider using CBPs as sites for teacher preparation.

CHALLENGING THE MYTHS: PREPARING CULTURALLY RESPONSIVE TEACHERS FOR AFRICAN AMERICAN STUDENTS

Undoubtedly, one of the most prominently expressed goals in many teacher education programs is the preparation of teachers who can teach every child effectively. However, the kind of training such a teacher would need to receive is often vaguely articulated. Teacher educator Ladson-Billings argues that an effective teacher of African American students must exhibit three characteristics she associates with culturally responsive pedagogy: emphasis on academic achievement, cultural competence, and sociopolitical critique.[25] Teachers who emphasize academic rigor among African American students operate in the belief that all students can learn.

Their cultural competency allows them to be confident, at ease, no-non-sense teachers who "take care of business" and have positive relationships with their students in and out of school. Culturally responsive teachers also seek to connect, rather than alienate, students from their cultural spaces by engaging in meaningful pedagogy imbued with sociopolitical consciousness. A culturally responsive pedagogy suggests that teachers need to be thoroughly conversant with their students' lives, not just in the context of the classroom or school, but also in their communities. Using CBPs as a gateway to the African American communities is a viable way to develop in preservice teachers the consciousness suggested by the culturally responsive pedagogical model. More importantly, CBPs provide education programs and departments in institutions of higher learning with opportunities to develop initiatives in African American communities that are aligned with the notion of the engaged campus.[26] Healthy engagement can lead to the fracturing of myths often associated with the cultural Other.

Myths shared by both university- and school-based educators that may explain the exclusion of African American CBPs as sites for community engagement and teacher education can be divided into two categories. The first category includes explanations that defend cultural neutrality in the practice of schooling and a belief in "best-practice" models that are abstracted from the knowledge of students' sociocultural, political, and historical realities. This perspective may include beliefs that educators know the child well, based solely on the interaction in the classrooms;[27] that educators engage in culturally neutral practices and there is no need to understand communities to which they do not belong;[28] and that educators can engage in culturally responsive pedagogy by simply adding information they deem true about other cultures without a deep knowledge of the target community of color.[29] The claim to value and cultural neutrality of schooling is problematic at best. Giroux urges educators to view schooling and knowledge as "neither neutral nor objective and, instead, to view it as a social construction embodying particular interests and assumptions."[30] Educators who understand that competing values are enacted every day in schooling practices are more likely to engage in culturally responsive pedagogy.

The second category of myths includes beliefs based on the deficit theory of culture and pathological perspectives about African American communities. Within these perspectives, educators' beliefs may include the views that CBPs are peripheral to the education of African American students;[31] that African American families and communities are not involved in the education of their children;[32] that interacting with African American communities is uncomfortable and should evoke fear among educators;[33] that African American communities are complex and relationships with them often get loud, complicated, messy, or political;[34] and that African American communities lack cultural funds of knowledge.[35] In contrast to these sentiments, many African American educators underscore the important role played by community-based initiatives in the education of African American students, both in the past and currently.

A look at Black education in the United States reveals that these myths are hardly supported by historical evidence. Education through self-help community initiatives, as well as culturally responsive pedagogy, are not new in African American communities. James Comer observed that "there has been a long-standing self-help tradition in the African American community," and that a strong desire to provide better conditions for their children has historically driven social change in African American communities.[36] Realizing the need to rally community efforts to promote the educational welfare of their children amid a majority culture that seems to care little for their success, African American communities have a track record of educational initiatives by and for African Americans dating back to slavery. Williams's study of the history of African American education in slavery and freedom examined the clandestine places and ways in which slaves organized their education, and how acquiring education became a symbol of resistance.[37] Royster described the Sabbath Schools, common soon after slavery, that were run predominantly by African Americans for African Americans.[38] These schools offered free instruction long before the advent of "public" or "free" education and were operated on weekends; they reached thousands of students who could not attend the weekday schools.[39] Freedom Schools, popular during the Civil Rights era, would continue the self-help educational charge among African American communities.[40] Hoover chronicled the African American independent schools during this era, including The Nairobi Day School in Palo Alto, California; the Center for Black Education in Washington, DC; the African Free School in Newark, New Jersey; Uhuru Sasa in New York City; and Malcolm X University in Durham, North Carolina.[41] More recently, Afrocentric and African-centered schools continue to offer models for education targeting the African American child within public, independent, and charter school contexts.[42]

African American educational initiatives, whether in the context of CBPs or in more formalized contexts such as those outlined above, have common threads weaving through them that are relevant here. One is the belief among African American communities that African American children are often not well served by the prevailing educational system. Another thread suggests that African American communities are an alternative site in which educational activity takes place. The third points to the need for educational reformers to take community-based educational initiatives seriously in their efforts toward equitable education and culturally responsive teacher education. Looking at what CBPs already do, institutions of higher learning should find ways of building on these strengths rather than treating African American communities as "pockets of needs, laboratories of experimentation, or passive recipients of expertise."[43]

MSL IN TEACHER EDUCATION:
POSSIBILITIES AND CHALLENGES

Teacher educators have decried the scarcity of opportunities and programs that prepare teachers to teach African American students. Ladson-Billings and Seidl and Friend spoke to this scarcity in detail.[44] Although I am not suggesting that immersion experiences in African American communities, as presented in the MSL approach, are in and of themselves sufficient to prepare teachers of African American students, I want to emphasize that they are an important step. As a concept and a practice, MSL has steadily gained popularity since the 1980s.[45] It can be argued that MSL currently stands as a substitute in the absence of significant efforts to educate, support, and sustain teachers committed to the education of African American students. Its appeal among teacher educators concerned with developing teachers capable of and willing to engage in culturally responsive pedagogy for African American students is that it seeks to embrace the "assets model" and avoids engaging in the voyeuristic, sensationalized, and "tourist" approach that is characteristic of many service-learning experiences in communities of color.[46] MSL also emphasizes the goals of multicultural understanding, community building, and social critique.[47] Most important, MSL emphasizes that race and ethnicity must be placed front and center in teacher education.

Seidl and Friend described the efforts of their teacher education graduate program at Ohio State University to partner with Mt. Olivet Baptist Community, which is predominantly African American. The program requires preservice teachers to engage in a community-based internship, which involves "working for two to three hours a week across the entire academic year with adults from the Mt. Olivet community in planning and implementing a number of different programs for children within the community."[48] Preservice teachers offer after-school homework help as well as reading and math tutorials. They also work with Sunday school classes, and participate in a community unity circle, in which community members discuss political, spiritual, and social concerns. Seidl and Friend reported that through this yearlong service-learning experience, participating preservice teachers have gained deeper understandings regarding cultural and the sociopolitical viewpoints of the African American communities they have interacted with. They have also gained a more nuanced understanding of racism. The course also helped build more trusting relationships between the campus and the surrounding community—two communities that have traditionally been divided.

Boyle-Baise described a one-credit-hour service-learning experience for preservice teachers that was linked to a three-credit-hour multicultural education course. Preservice teachers, who were predominantly White, were required to spend twenty hours service-learning in churches and community organizations serving low-income communities of color, including African American communities. The college instructor facilitating the service-learning had collaborated with leaders of the various community organizations to develop a service-learning program that was based on mutuality, shared control, and respect for communities. She noted, "Our partnership included two pastors, one for a racially mixed congregation, the other for a predominantly Black church; a director of university program for students of color and education director for the Black church; the program director for the Boys and Girls Club; the director of a community center; the parent coordinator for Head Start; and a teacher education professor."[49] The service-learning component afforded preservice teachers opportunities to become acquainted with culturally and economically diverse communities. It also allowed preservice teachers to situate children within family and community life, and to identify assets and resources within the communities. Boyle-Baise noted that despite the immersion experience and the reduction of stereotypes that resulted, the preservice teachers' understanding and social and institutionalized inequalities remained elusive.

In her education courses for preservice teachers, Sleeter engages her preservice teachers in service-learning in several community centers, churches, and the Boys and Girls Club. She chooses community centers that are staffed by people from the community. After their interaction with students, parents, and community members in the community centers, Sleeter reported that her students who were predominantly White gained a deeper understanding in key areas that will most likely impact their future teaching of African America students. For instance, they compared the conversational and interaction patterns present in community sites to patterns often privileged in mainstream classrooms. They also interacted with African American parents from low-income backgrounds and learned of the parents' educational aspirations for their children. Additionally, they observed the skills and abilities that African American children use in church or community centers that "suggest a higher level of responsibility, as well as cognitive knowledge and/or linguistic skills, than the children display in classrooms."[50]

What these examples highlight are some key tenets of MSL. Multicultural service-learning demands that prospective teachers participate in carefully designed community-based service-learning experiences that allow them to interact with communities of color and engage in community-building activities in their service-learning sites. Most important, however, is the reflection and learning that results from purposeful engagement with these communities. The benefits of this Freirean notion of praxis for both prospective teachers and communities are wide ranging. Purposeful engagement provides opportunities for prospective teachers to reconsider deficit or supremacy views,[51] fracture the essentialist positions that define African Americans in simplistic and stereotypical terms,[52] gain an appreciation for sociopolitical complexities that face African Americans in their contexts and limit their engagement in school tasks,[53] learn to appreciate the community wisdom, strengths, and resources, and gain a deeper understanding of sociopolitical critique and action.[54] The obvious challenge that MSL faces as a new field is that it has yet to develop a supporting, comprehensive research base that shows its impact among preservice teachers. More research is needed to show ways in which MSL can develop the skills, knowledge, and dispositions needed to become effective teachers of African American students. Perhaps the biggest challenge facing MSL in teacher education programs is a lack of institutionalization. Multicultural service-learning is largely regarded as an "add-on" experience, even in programs that encourage a series of field experiences for their teacher candidates. In addition, many teacher educators—even those who do not subscribe to the myths outlined earlier—find that establishing sustainable relationships with CBPs is a daunting task.

ENHANCING MULTICULTURAL SERVICE-LEARNING THROUGH DEVELOPING PURPOSEFUL CAMPUS-CBP PARTNERSHIPS

I have argued in this chapter that MSL experiences should be encouraged in teacher education programs that seek to prepare culturally responsive teachers of African American students. This would involve changes on two fronts: a broadened definition of community partnerships and relationship building with African American CBPs. Education faculty in institutions of higher learning must broaden the definition of community partnerships to include CBPs. In this broadened sense of partnerships, MSL, as described in this chapter, would become a core rather than peripheral field experience alongside the traditional school-based field experiences. Such a move is both political and pedagogical, and it forces departments of education to examine institutionalized mechanisms that have served to validate some knowledges and cultures and exclude others. It also demands that faculty members form working, if not collaborative, relationships with other offices and programs on campus that would not normally have strong links with education departments. Since adding MSL to my courses, I have found myself working closely not just with faculty in other academic disciplines, but also with campus offices that offer the logistical support needed to establish sustainable relationships with communities. Last, institutionalizing MSL would need to be accompanied by an alignment with the reward systems. Multicultural service-learning, like other community service-learning experiences, require a great deal of work from faculty to organize and operate.

Building healthy relationships with CBPs is vital to the institutionalization of MSL. Literature emphasizes that good relationships with community are based on (1) common goals, (2) mutual trust and collaboration, and (3) being mindful of history and power differentials. Langseth explores literature and stresses that three myths must be addressed in order to preserve campus–community collaboration: (1) there exists superior and deficient cultures; (2) there is superior knowledge and experience in higher education as compared to the communities; and (3) there is a hierarchy of wisdom, with faculty wiser than students and students wiser than community.[55] These myths, among others, prevent a healthy engagement between education faculty and CBPs. A paradigm shift must occur to allow for the development of a mutually beneficial relationship. At the core of this paradigm shift must be the willingness to share the "expert" role with community members who know their children best. The conviction that communities are committed and knowledgeable only happens when education faculty gain deep, rather than superficial, knowledge of the community. Such knowledge leads to the embracing of the "assets model" that suggests an orientation of "doing with" rather than "doing for."[56] Taken together, the broad-based programmatic change in departments of education suggested here would go a long way toward institutionalizing MSL.

CONCLUSION

Educating America's diverse K–12 students demands that institutions of higher learning prepare teachers who are deeply knowledgeable and skilled in teaching all students. For effective teaching to occur, teachers must gain experience in cultures other than their own. Multicultural service-learning, with its emphasis on learning in community-based contexts involving communities of color, offers the opportunity for prospective teachers to gain this vital experience. In this chapter, I have explained why MSL in African American communities makes sense. However, I must acknowledge that embracing MSL with African American or other ethnic or racially based CBPs is not consistent with the typical teacher education program. Teacher educators do see value in their students' service-learning and interning in schools. Few, however, see the need to extend beyond the school into the larger community. Yet, available research tells us that teachers' perceptions of students' culture and communities influences the way they teach, particularly with African American communities. In its emphasis on learning about diversity through active engagement with diverse communities, MSL promotes a fundamental tenet of a community-engaged teacher education. Essentially both demand that to produce proficient teachers in the twenty-first century, education faculty must undertake programmatic initiatives and changes on their campuses and commit to the development of healthy community-based learning experiences.

NOTES

1. This chapter was first published in Stephanie Y. Evans, Colette M. Taylor, Michelle R. Dunlap, DeMond S. Miller, eds., *African Americans and Community Engagement in Higher Education: Community Service, Service-learning, and Community-based Research* (Albany: State University of New York Press, 2009).

2. Linda Darling-Hammond, *Professional Development Schools: Schools for Developing a Profession* (New York: Teachers College Press, 1994).

3. See Marilynne Boyle-Baise, *Multicultural Service-Learning* (New York: Teachers College Press, 2002); Marilynne Boyle-Baise, Bart Epler, William McCoy, "Shared Control: Community Voices in Multicultural Service Learning," *The Educational Forum* 65, no. 4 (2001): 344–53; Christine Sleeter, "Strengthening Multicultural Education with Community-Based Learning" in *Integrating Service-Learning and Multicultural Education in Colleges and Universities*, ed. Carolyn R. O'Grady (Mahwah, NJ: Lawrence Erlbaum Associates, 2000), 263–76; Gloria Ladson-Billings, "Fighting for Our Lives: Preparing Teachers to Teach African American Students," *Journal of Teacher Education* 51, no. 3 (2000): 206–14.

4. Peter C. Murrell, Jr., *African-Centered Pedagogy: Developing Schools of Achievement for African American Children* (Albany: State University of New York Press, 2002), xxxviii.

5. James Comer, "The Potential Effects of Community Organizations on the Future of Our Youth," *Teacher's College Record* 94, no. 3 (1993): 658–61.

6. Shirley Brice Heath and Milbrey W. McLaughlin, "Community Organizations as Family: Endeavors That Engage and Support Adolescents," *Phi Delta Kappan* 72, no. 8 (1991): 623–27.

7. Gloria Ladson-Billings, "Fighting for Our Lives."

8. Arnetha F. Ball, "Empowering Pedagogies That Enhance Multicultural Students," *Teachers College Record* 102, no. 6 (2000): 1006–34.

9. Peter C. Murrell, Jr., *African-Centered Pedagogy*.

10. Wade A. Boykin, Robert J. Jagers, Constance M. Ellison, and Aretha Albury, "Communalism: Conceptualization and Measurement of an Afrocultural Social Orientation," *Journal of Black Studies* 27, no. 3 (1997): 409–18.

11. Arnetha F. Ball and Ted Lardner, *African American Literacies Unleashed: Vernacular English and the Composition Class* (Carbondale, IL: Southern Illinois University Press, 2005).

12. Arnetha F. Ball and Ted Lardner, *African American Literacies Unleashed.*

13. Nsenga Warfield-Coppock, "The Rites of Passage Movement: A Resurgence of African-Centered Practices for Socializing African American Youth," *Journal of Negro Education* 61, no. 4 (1992): 471–82.

14. Aminifu R. Harvey, "An After-School Manhood Development Program," in *Educating Our Black Children: New Directions and Radical Approaches*, ed. Richard Majors (New York: Routledge Falmer, 2001), 157–68.

15. Cynthia M. Silva, Robert P. Moses, Parker Johnson, and Jacqueline Rivers, "The Algebra Project: Making School Mathematics Count," *Journal of Negro Education* 59, no. 3 (1990): 37–91.

16. Julia Cass, "The Moses Factor," http://www.typp.org/media/docs/6245_TheMosesFactor(motherjones).pdf (accessed January 31, 2007).

17. Roubbins Jamal LaMothe, *Uncharted Territories: Past, Present, and Future* (Somerville, MA: Books of Hope Press, 2001).

18. Doug Holder, "Books of Hope Brings the Writer Out in Somerville Youth," 2008, http://somervillenews.typepad.com/thesomervillenews/2008/08/books-of-hope-b.html (accessed April 2009).

19. Amy E. Busch and Arnetha F. Ball, "Lifting Voices in the City," *Educational Leadership* 62, no. 2 (2002): 64–67.

20. Personal communication with the program coordinators.

21. Stephanie Y. Evans, "Preface: Using History, Experience, and Theory to Balance Relationships in Community Engagement," in *African Americans and Community Engagement in Higher Education*, ix-xxii.

22. Patricia M. Cooper, "Effective White Teachers of Black Children: Teaching Within a Community," *Journal of Teacher Education* 54, no. 95 (2003): 413–27.

23. Gloria Ladson-Billings, "Fighting for Our Lives," 206

24. See exceptions discussed in Christine Sleeter, "Preparing White Teachers for Diverse Students," in *Handbook of Research on Teacher Education: Enduring Questions in Changing Contexts*, ed. Marilyn Cochran-Smith, Sharon Feiman-Nemser, D. John McIntyre, and Kelly Demers (New York: Routledge and Association of Teacher Educators, 2008), 551–58.

25. Gloria Ladson-Billings, "Fighting for Our Lives."

26. Ernest L. Boyer, "The Scholarship of Engagement." *Journal of Public Service and Outreach* 1, no. 1 (1996): 11–20; "Creating the New American College," *The Chronicle of Higher Education* 40, no. 27 (1994): A48.

27. Marilynne Boyle-Baise, *Multicultural Service-Learning.*

28. Christine Sleeter, "Strengthening Multicultural Education."

29. Marilynne Boyle-Baise, *Multicultural Service-Learning.*

30. Henry Giroux, *Teachers as Intellectuals: Toward a Critical Pedagogy of Learning* (Westport, CT: Bergin & Garvey Publishers, Inc., 1988), 7.

31. Amy E. Busch and Arnetha F. Ball, "Lifting Voices in the City."

32. Gail L. Thompson, *What African American Parents Want Educators to Know* (Westport, CT: Praeger, 2003).

33. Barbara Seidl and Gloria Friend, "The Unification of Church and State."

34. Gail L. Thompson, *Through Ebony Eyes* (San Francisco, CA: Jossey-Bass, 2004).

35. Carol D. Lee, "The State of Knowledge about the Education of African Americans," in *Black Education: A Transformative Research and Action Agenda for The New Century*, ed. Joyce E. King (Mahwah, NJ: Lawrence Erlbaum Associates, 2005), 45–71.

36. James P. Comer, *Waiting for a Miracle: Why Schools Can't Solve Our Problems—and How We Can* (New York: Plume, 1998).

37. Heather A. Williams, *Self-Taught: African American Education in Slavery and Freedom* (Chapel Hill: University of North Carolina Press, 2005), 11.

38. Jacqueline Jones Royster, *Traces of a Stream: Literacy and Social Change among African American Women* (Pittsburgh, PA: University of Pittsburgh Press, 2000).

39. James D. Anderson, *The Education of Blacks in the South 1860–1935* (Chapel Hill: University of North Carolina Press, 1988).

40. Joyce E. King and Sharon Parker, "A Detroit Conversation," in *Black Education: A Transformative Research and Action Agenda for the New Century*, ed. Joyce E. King (Mahwah, NJ: Lawrence Erlbaum Associates, 2005), 243–60.

41. Mary Eleanor Rhodes Hoover, "The Nairobi Day School: An American Independent School 1966–1984," *Journal of Negro Education* 61, no. 2 (1992): 201–10.

42. For information on Afrocentric schools and African-centered schools, see Molefi K. Asante, *The Afrocentric Idea* (Philadelphia, PA: Temple University Press, 1987); Diane S. Pollard and Cheryl S. Ajirotutu, *African-Centered Schooling in Theory and Practice* (Westport, CT: Bergin & Garvey Publishers, Inc., 2000); Murrell, Peter C., Jr., *African-Centered Pedagogy*.

43. Robert G. Bringle, Richard Games, and Edward A. Malloy, *Colleges and Universities as Citizens* (Boston: Allyn and Bacon, 1999), 9.

44. Gloria Ladson-Billings, "Culturally Relevant Pedagogy in African-Centered Schools: Possibilities for Progressive Educational Reform," in *African-Centered Schooling in Theory and Practice*, ed. Diane. S. Pollard and Cheryl. S. Ajirotutu (Westport, CT: Bergin & Garvey Publishers, Inc, 2000), 187–98; Barbara Seidl and Gloria Friend, "The Unification of Church and State."

45. Marilynne Boyle-Baise, *Multicultural Service-Learning*; Carolyn R. O'Grady, *Integrating Service-Learning and Multicultural Education in Colleges and Universities*.

46. Marilynne Boyle-Baise, *Multicultural Service-Learning*; Christine Sleeter, "Strengthening Multicultural Education."

47. Marilynne Boyle-Baise, *Multicultural Service-Learning*; Michelle R. Dunlap, "Voices of Students in Multicultural Service-Learning Settings," *Michigan Journal of Community Service Learning* (Fall 1998): 58–67.

48. Barbara Seidl and Gloria Friend, "The Unification of Church and State," 149.

49. Marilynne Boyle-Baise, *Multicultural Service-Learning*, 78.

50. Christine Sleeter, "Strengthening Multicultural Education," 270.

51. Marilynne Boyle-Baise and Patricia Efiom, "The Construction of Meaning: Learning from Service-Learning," in *Integrating Service-Learning and Multicultural Education in Colleges and Universities*, ed. Carolyn R. O'Grady (Mahwah, NJ: Lawrence Erlbaum Associates, 2000), 209–26.

52. Gloria Ladson-Billings, "Culturally Relevant Pedagogy in African-Centered Schools"; Shirley Brice Heath, "Island by Island We Must Cross: Challenges from Language and Culture among African Americans," in *African-Centered Schooling in Theory and Practice*, 163–86.

53. Gloria Ladson-Billings, "Culturally Relevant Pedagogy."

54. Christine Sleeter, "Strengthening Multicultural Education"; Gloria Ladson-Billings, "Fighting for Our Lives"; Marilynne Boyle-Baise, Bart Epler, William McCoy, "Shared Control: Community Voices in Multicultural Service Learning," *The Educational Forum* 65, no. 4 (2001): 344–53.

55. Mark Langseth, "Maximizing Impact, Minimizing Harm: Why Service-Learning Must More Fully Integrate Multicultural Education," in *Integrating Service-Learning and Multicultural Education in Colleges and Universities*, ed. Carolyn R. O'Grady (Mahwah, NJ: Lawrence Erlbaum Associates, 2000), 45–71.

56. Kelly Ward and Lisa Wolf-Wendel, "Community-Centered Service Learning," *American Behavioral Scientist* 43, no. 5 (2000): 767–80.

4

❦

Lessons Learned in the Field about Healthy Campus-Community Partnerships

Any writing on educating teachers for diversity will mention the importance of community field experiences (CFEs) that are based on collaboration between the campus and diverse communities. But few include details on how such collaborations are designed, implemented, or sustained. Even fewer speak to the importance of looking at these collaborations in the contexts of campus-wide efforts for developing campus-community partnerships. In this chapter, I focus on the issue of campus-community partnerships in a broader sense, focusing on how they can be formed and sustained. In doing this, I draw mainly on my experience working on the emerging campus-community partnership between Smith College, a private liberal arts college, and Hillcrest, an economically distressed urban community in the Northeastern part of the United States.[1] Early on in my work with this partnership, I decided to use my experience as a participant observer to better understand the process of developing healthy campus-community partnerships among these two entities. The literature suggests that despite the upsurge of the "community engagement movement" in institutions of higher learning since the 1990s, while college-community partnerships have increased, they have also tended to reinforce and sustain the traditional hegemony of academia and the marginalization of economically depressed communities (often urban and inhabited by persons of color). It also suggests that small liberal arts colleges, especially, face challenges when it comes to increasing their community engagement with "distant" communities. I asked, "What factors can facilitate the creation of healthy campus-community partnerships among small liberal arts colleges and poor, urban communities of color? What are the characteristics of such partnerships?" I began to pay attention to ways that the principles of successful campus-community partnerships articulated by Strand et al.[2] were present in the Smith-Hillcrest partnership. In this chapter, I discuss the Smith-Hillcrest partnership and note that in many ways it resembles many efforts in small liberal arts colleges since the 1990s to promote community engagement: it is small in scale, and the impetus for its development rests on a few key campus and community players who strongly believe in campus-community connections. These campus players span the disciplines, including education. I outline six factors that I believe have strengthened the Smith-Hillcrest partnership, underlining the lessons that can be learned about healthy campus-community partnerships from this emerging partnership. Lastly, I propose a new understanding of healthy campus-community partnerships as dialogue and conclude that such a conceptualization can provide us with a vocabulary with which to further explore this issue at the college level and in teacher education.

DEVELOPING A HEALTHY CAMPUS-COMMUNITY PARTNERSHIP: BACKGROUND AND PARTICIPANTS

In this section I describe the Smith-Hillcrest partnership as an example of a current effort at Smith College that indicates a growing interest in community engagement work. From the perspective of a participant observer,[3] I provide the contextual background, introduce community partners, explain my role, and introduce the general and specific goals of the Smith-Hillcrest partnership. I highlight lessons about healthy campus-community partnerships that could be learned from the Smith-Hillcrest partnership through a discussion of six factors that I believe have helped shape this emerging partnership. My Smith colleagues and I were introduced to the Hillcrest community by the principal of the Torres Elementary School in 2005. Three years previously, I and a colleague in the Department of Education and Child Study, as well the director in the Smith College Office of Educational Outreach, met with the principal of Torres to discuss opportunities to enhance learning among Smith and Torres students. Although the urban school and the Hillcrest community in which it is located are just seventeen miles south of the small-town college, they are "distant" due to differences marked by class and culture, as well as environment. At that time, the college had only a limited connection with this distant community. The initial visit with the principal impressed on us the dire situation in which the school was operating and the urgency for change. On one hand, this K–5 school had consistently registered low educational achievement scores and a high poverty rate (over 85 percent of students were considered low-income) among its over 700 students, according to the No Child Left Behind Report Card. In 2003, for example, the school was designated as underperforming by the Massachusetts Commissioner of Education. On the other hand, the state mandated compliance with state and national standards and provided little of the money and resources that would make meeting such demands possible. With the support of the Smith College president, an institutional partnership was forged that encouraged Smith faculty and students to work closely with Torres Elementary. In subsequent meetings, the school principal insisted that the academic programs resulting from the partnerships should not operate in a vacuum, and that to substantially address the root cause of the problems facing his school, a broader partnership was needed that would focus on the well-being of the entire Hillcrest community. He noted the glaring educational, economic, and social disparities that existed in Hillcrest as compared to other areas in the city, and urged for a partnership that would recognize the school as being inextricably linked with the community and its challenges. His view of the role of the college reminded me of Ernest Boyer's[4] challenge to the institution of higher learning to engage with communities in systemic and comprehensive ways by connecting its resources "to our most pressing social, civic, and ethical problems, to our children, to our teachers, and to our cities."[5] The principal advocated for stronger links between Smith College and the Hillcrest schools and community around a wide range of issues. He suggested that the Hillcrest Outreach Network (HON) would be an ideal community partner.

HON was formed in 1996, when four innovative community-based organizations teamed with local activists to form a coalition to combat the challenges facing Hillcrest. At its formation, it was expected that HON would be the outreach arm of the founding member organizations, but HON quickly evolved to become the established outreach mechanism for the entire Hillcrest community. With a sophisticated network in place, HON aims to provide an "organizational, human, and technological infrastructure to bring families, businesses, schools, other neighborhood institutions, and individuals into the collective life of the [Hillcrest] community."[6] In addition, HON uses a "population based" approach, with the goal of reaching out to each resident through the door-to-door work of community members who are trained in outreach, community health development, and organizing. Each worker is assigned to one of the ten geographic zones in Hillcrest, and each zone comprises approximately 1,000 people. HON offers information, referrals, education, and support services to the residents of Hillcrest. Because of its access to the community, the area schools and other service agencies have come to rely on HON to facilitate their work in Hillcrest.[7]

Hillcrest, with a population of approximately 11,000 (75 percent of which is Puerto Rican), has one of the lowest per capita incomes in the state and is home to one public middle school (Blake) and three elementary schools, including Torres. When compared to other areas in the city and the state in general, Hillcrest records disproportionately low levels of academic attainment and household median income, and high levels of environmentally related diseases, HIV/AIDS, gang activity, incarceration, students on free or reduced lunch, and failing Massachusetts Comprehensive Assessment System (MCAS) test scores. However, as many in Hillcrest are likely to point out, it is not these challenges that make their community unique—the same characteristics can be found in almost every poor urban location in the United States. Rather, it is the residents' sense of family and community, pride in their culture, history of activism, and commitment to a community-involvement approach to solving problems. The HON embodies this outlook. So does the Hillcrest Campus Committee (HCC), a major decision-maker in Hillcrest.[8]

The HCC, of which HON is a member, meets monthly and has representation from Hillcrest residents, service agencies, four public schools, and partnering institutions. The close affinity between the two had implications for the kind of partnership Smith College would have with Hillcrest. First, because the same individuals occupy leadership roles in HON and HCC and there is high resemblance in their goals, philosophy, history, and vision. Partnering with HON also meant working closely with HCC. Second, in 2003 HON and HCC developed the Hillcrest Strategic Plan, which addressed four major goal areas: lifelong learning, economic development, health, and safety. Lifelong learning (and specifically, literacy), would become a central focus of the Smith-Hillcrest partnership. Third, both HON and the HCC subscribe to the Campus Concept ideology, which as the current co-chairman of HCC explained, is the idea that "our schools are public buildings and by bringing the entire community into our schools, we not only make the best use of public space, we bring our families together with our children in lifelong learning and engagement in many areas of community life."[9] The campus concept ideology has a long history in Hillcrest, and can be traced back to the 1950s with the HCC's battles against urban renewal initiatives and to retain needed services (including schools) in Hillcrest.[10] Today, the campus concept ideology is supported by numerous community-based organizations and community residents, and it would also influence the Smith-Hillcrest partnership. At the moment of Smith's entry into Hillcrest, the HON and

HCC leadership was concerned about improving the well-being of Hillcrest adult residents and students through literacy, among other interventions. However, it was not immediately clear to the nine Smith faculty and staff (who had thus far indicated interest in partnering with Hillcrest) the role the community leaders expected them to play in this process.[11]

SOME INDICATORS OF HEALTHY
CAMPUS-COMMUNITY PARTNERSHIPS:
EXAMPLES FROM AN EMERGING PARTNERSHIP

Strand et al. rightly insists that the type of entry, the manner of conducting partnership activities, and types of outcomes resulting from a partnership can serve as indicators of successful campus-community partnerships. In healthy partnerships with community, the entry is characterized by a shared worldview and agreement about goals in addition to trust and mutual respect among partners. Campus and community partners also conduct partnership activities in a manner that is flexible and attentive to issues of power and effective communication. Finally, campus and community partners seek to satisfy each other's interests or needs, have their organizational capacities enhanced and together adopt long-range social change perspectives through partnership. In this section I discuss six features that characterized the Smith-Hillcrest partnership in its first two years of existence that I believe are indicators of a healthy campus-community partnership. These are: (1) careful entry; (2) negotiating power and establishing mutuality; (3) capacity building; (4) focus on community needs; (5) satisfying immediate distinct needs and interests; and (6) embracing long-range social change perspectives.[12]

(1) Campus partners engaged in careful entry

The campus partners in the Smith-Hillcrest partnership recognized that before they could enter into a meaningful partnership, they had to become better informed about the needs of their community partners. They participated in numerous meetings with the principal of Torres and other community leaders, as well as trips to learn more about the Hillcrest community. Over time, Smith faculty and staff became familiar guests in HON offices and Torres Elementary, and regular participants in monthly community meetings organized by the HCC. These conversations and visits provided opportunities for community and campus partners to develop a shared worldview, clarify goals of the partnership, and cultivate trust and mutual respect.

(2) Negotiating power and establishing mutuality: Obtaining a grant

A significant "partnership moment" occurred and traditional campus/ community barriers were broken while collaboratively writing a grant to lay out the infrastructure for the partnership. Through a series of meetings involving Smith faculty and staff and Hillcrest community members, a successful application was made for a Cooperative Conference Grant (U13) through the National Institutes of Health (NIH) for a three-year grant that would support the college-community partnership. The limited funds through this grant were expected to be spent developing relationships rather than on developing a single program. An organizing committee (OC) held monthly meetings to chart the structure of the partnership, and most of its members continue to meet. The OC consisted of seven Smith faculty and staff members, four HON and HCC members, two Torres Elementary representatives, and five representatives of neighborhood service-providing agencies. Early meetings resulted in the articulation of some general and specific goals. The overarching goal was to nurture a healthy relationship between the college and community that would be sustainable, mutually beneficial to the stakeholders, and aimed at using the community-based participatory research (CBPR) approach to address the enduring challenges facing Hillcrest.[13] The following were objectives of the partnership:

- To establish an academic-community research partnership, through intensive meetings and discussions among Smith outreach staff and faculty researchers, Torres Elementary, and the leadership of HON;
- to use the academic-community research partnership to elucidate existing barriers to engagement in supportive services for those at risk in the Hillcrest community;
- to devise strategies for eliminating barriers to engagement for those at risk in the community;
- to employ these strategies to engage a broad spectrum of Hillcrest residents in the development and implementation of a community family literacy center;
- to work in partnership with Hillcrest residents to evaluate initial success of the family literacy center; and
- to identify long-term research goals so that further knowledge gained through basic research may be applied to address literacy needs in the Hillcrest community.

This initial collaborative grant-writing process allowed for campus and community partners to develop mutual goals, increase trust, and facilitate shared decision making. Community partners, especially, developed more ownership of the partnership and felt equally responsible for influencing its direction.

(3) Enhancing organizational capacities of the community partners: Stabilizing the HON database

From the beginning, the partnership understood the responsibility of enhancing the organizational capacities of HON. Instability at HON was mainly due to issues related to the physical structure of the office space and partly due to outdated technology. The state of the HON database did not allow for optimal use of data that had been collected over the years on about half of the Hillcrest population and its needs. At the time, HON was operating with a fraction of its optimal personnel. In an ideal situation, HON workers would enter into a central database the demographic and referral information on all residents in their geographic zones. The partnership agreed that improvement and stabilization of HON's data management capabilities was a priority, and Smith College Information Technology Services staff members were invited to help. Smith donated and installed a new server and related software for this purpose. Further, members of the partnership worked closely with the Smith Institutional Review Board to streamline HON's information collection procedures (including the Referral Form, informed consent, and human subjects paperwork) and to bring HON into alignment with federal guidelines. One other effort undertaken by a community member of the partnership to expand HON's capabilities involved compiling a resource guide featuring descriptions of the services, targeted populations, and contact information of twenty-one major service providers in the area. These activities show both community and college leveraging the resources in the two sites to enhance the capacity of the community partner.

(4) Focusing on the needs of the community: Community forums and research

From the outset, the goals of the Smith-Hillcrest partnership emphasized a focus on researching and addressing community needs around literacy. In May 2006, the partnership sponsored a community-wide Education Festival that was held at Torres Elementary. The event attracted over 250 residents and was broadcast on the local news. Activities included displays by local artists, a community dinner, and visits to booths set up by numerous literacy service agencies throughout the city. Residents also participated in a discussion about the proposed family literacy center and expressed their hopes for services, including computer classes and supportive workshops on parenting.

Other efforts to include residents' voices included a pilot study—
"Elucidating Barriers to Literacy Study"—that was completed in two
phases. The first phase involved a survey that was administered orally
to residents of Hillcrest to determine residents' perceptions of their involvement in education-related services, barriers to involvement in these
services, and interest in adult education opportunities. The survey also
sought to explore residents' perceptions of common ways in which they
receive information about community events in Hillcrest. This information would be useful in the development and implementation of the proposed community family literacy center. The 147 respondents were Hillcrest residents who, according to HON records, had not previously been
formally "reached" through the door-to-door outreach activities of HON
workers. As a result of this research, this population was introduced to
the wide array of services offered through HON. According to the director of HON, the organization had, at that time, been able to reach only
about half of the targeted population, mainly due to inadequate personnel and infrastructure at the organization.

In the second phase of the pilot study, I worked closely with HON workers to design, conduct, and analyze data from nine focus groups. Seven of
these were with residents from nine out of ten geographic zones of Hillcrest. The focus group discussions were framed around the same questions
that were contained in the residents' survey. About fifty residents participated in the seven focus groups. The eighth focus group was comprised of
six school-related individuals (teachers, school-based after-school service
providers, guidance counselors, etc.), while the final focus group consisted
of twelve representatives from agencies and community-based organizations offering education and related services (such as ESOL, GED, library,
adult basic education, and after-school programs not run by the schools).
The discussion with school personnel and service providers centered
around their perceptions of barriers facing Hillcrest residents and ideas on
how a community literacy center might help reduce these barriers.

For the interviews, I provided HON workers with the training they
needed on conducting focus groups. All sessions were audio-taped, and
were conducted in Spanish when necessary. I oversaw the transcription,
translation, management, and analyses of the data with the help of Smith
students. Data from focus groups were analyzed using the constant com-
parison method to identify major themes or ideas.[14] A draft of our analyses was first sent to HON researchers and then other partnership members as a way to check for accuracy and solicit critique and feedback. The
results of the pilot study[15] confirmed that lifelong learning and literacy
remain a high priority in Hillcrest. They explicated the need for urgent
intervention to provide programming in high-priority areas, including
computer literacy, ESL/ESOL, job skills education, and GED. It became

clear that any programming for the center should include mechanisms to overcome identified barriers to engagement, such as language barriers and the lack of adequate transportation and child care.

(5) Satisfying immediate distinct needs: School-focused efforts

The school-based efforts, started in 2003 through a partnership between Smith and Torres Elementary and strengthened after the 2005 partnership with HON, are a good example of meeting the immediate needs of both school and college partners. Following the first meeting with the principal of Torres Elementary, it became apparent that the urgent need facing the school was to provide support to classroom teachers and in the after-school program. The Office of Educational Outreach organized an after-school program that has allowed numerous Smith students to volunteer at the school for two hours one to three days per week, providing home-work help and enrichment activities to first- through fifth-grade students at Torres. College students also volunteer as full-day teaching assistants at the Torres and Blake schools during January term, working alongside mentor teachers to boost the achievement of elementary and middle school students while gaining understanding of urban education issues. During this time, two Smith faculty members partnered with Torres and Blake schools to establish an innovative sports program that includes a tutoring/mentoring component. Education courses at Smith continue to use Hillcrest as a site for service learning. Additionally, the deepening relationship between Smith and Hillcrest led to summer programs for Hillcrest youth and teachers: the STEP UP program—a week-long resi-dential leadership development program for middle school girls—and week-long Summer Institutes for Educators, which offer enriching profes-sional development on the Smith College campus. Each summer, during the duration of my research, "25–40 [Torres] students were awarded full scholarships to attend the Smith-Northampton Summer School Program, where they took part in academic enrichment courses and recreational ac-tivities on the Smith College campus."[16] Probably as a result of increased exposure to the Hillcrest community, four 2007 graduates of the Smith College Teacher Education Program were employed as first-year teachers at Torres. These school-based activities have particularly helped meet the needs of Hillcrest school partners and Smith faculty and students.

(6) Embracing long-range social change perspectives: More grant-writing activities

The campus and community partners remain committed to the goal of securing physical space and implementing actual programming for the family literacy center. Toward this end, the OC has participated in the writing of several grants since the partnership's inception, although none had received funding by the time I completed my report. They have also written several grant proposals to support research between faculty and community members. At one point, the partnership invited a Smith College development officer to help write a grant; grant-writing efforts continue. In January 2008, for example, a community research grant proposal between HON and Smith College was sent to NIH. The goal of this proposed collaborative project is to document and assess the impact of using community narrative to address health disparities in the Hillcrest community, through a community-wide digital stories project. The digital stories project was started in 2004 by community activists, and has since been supported by HON as a tool for outreach and community-building. Clearly, securing adequate funding remains an important focus of this partnership.

An unexpected development in funding opportunities may bring the vision of a community literacy center closer to reality. Late in 2007, an announcement was made regarding funding through State Medical Center (SMC) to support programming at the campus center. SMC has been a major supporter of HON and the Hillcrest community over the years, and this time pledged a $2.8 million seven-year Community Benefits grant. The money will fund HON, among other things, and some of it is earmarked for small projects for which individuals or community-based organizations will apply. A steering committee comprised of HCC members, which will oversee the distribution of funds, began a series of meetings almost immediately, and part of its task is to develop the guidelines and bylaws that will determine the kinds of grant proposals it will accept. It is likely that programming supported through this grant will contribute to bringing the vision of a vibrant, literacy-rich, and engaged Hillcrest community closer to reality. It is also likely that the Smith-Hillcrest partnership will continue to play a key role in shaping the next steps for this community.

The six factors discussed above shed light on entry, process, and outcomes of the Smith-Hillcrest partnership in its early stages of development. As Strand et al. note, these three areas can be powerful indicators of successful or healthy campus-community partnerships. The entry into the Smith-Hillcrest partnership was carefully done and involved contact initiated by community leaders who clearly identified needs in their own community. The campus partners took time to acquire a deep knowledge of the community through conversations and frequent visits before engaging in any projects. The process of conducting the Smith-Hillcrest partnership involved a variety of initiatives that not only brought the partners closer in terms of shared vision, common goals, trust, and mutual respect, but also were flexible, focused, and collaborative. And finally the partnership allowed for partners' interests to emerge. Some of these were addressed while others await further funding. On the community side, HON had its capacity expanded through technology, research and grant-writing knowledge, and Torres students and teachers benefited from additional tutoring and coaching help that became available through school-based initiatives. Smith faculty and students benefited through service-learning, volunteering, internships, employment, and research. For college, community, and school partners, funding opportunities have opened up that allow them to entertain long-range social change initiatives through continued partnership. It remains to be seen how this young partnership evolves in the future. College and community partners with whom I spoke in December 2007 regarding their views of this partnership indicated that they would like to continue in the partnership. The community partners are eager for expanded and multifaceted collaborative projects with college partners. The campus partners do recognize that the partnership is in its early stages, and will need to grow and be further institutionalized within the college in order to sustain itself and have the desired impact.

HEALTHY COLLEGE-COMMUNITY PARTNERSHIPS CONCEPTUALIZED AS DIALOGUE

In reflecting on the salient lessons I have learned from a participant observer role in the partnership process outlined above, the conceptualization of healthy campus-community partnerships as dialogue seems fitting. Analysis by analogue, for all its limitations, has been used by others and found to be a useful approach to examine the nature and character of partnerships.[17] I use the term dialogue here in a Freirean way to indicate that partnerships, just like dialogue, are encounters between two or more players, mediated by social realities. According to Freire, dialogue is "an encounter between men, mediated by the world, in order to name the world." He adds:

> Because dialogue is an encounter among men who name the world, it must not be a situation where some men name on behalf of others. It is an act of creation; it must not serve as a crafty instrument of domination of one man by another. The domination implicit in dialogue is that of the world by the dialoguers; it is conquest of the world for the liberation of men.[18]

In using the Freirean notion of dialogue here to describe healthy campus-community partnerships, I am fully aware that I am transposing Freire's ideas from the original context in which he speaks to the educator-learner relationship in a specific social, political, and cultural context. Freire sees dialogue as an alternative to the traditional authoritarian relationship in what he calls the "banking education." I am using the notion of dialogue in a different context here, but I see distinct similarities, especially in the campus-community partnerships which are often characterized by expert-recipient attitude. Furthermore, as many scholars of Freire including Henry Giroux, Joe Kincheloe, Peter McLaren, and Ira Shor have urged, Freire's ideas are very applicable in our North American context. Freire, in the Foreword of *Paulo Freire: A Critical Encounter*, edited by Peter McLaren and Peter Leonard, applauds this recreating of his ideas and calls it "exceedingly productive work." In an interview with Shor, Freire suggests that his notion of educator-learner encompasses situations akin to campus-community contexts.

> Once, an intellectual tried to participate in the activities of a group of peasants. He went day after day to them, trying to become a kind of advisor. On the third or fourth day, one of the peasants told him, "Look comrade, if you think you come here to teach us how to cut down a tree, it is not necessary, because we already know how to do that. What we need to know from you is whether you will be with us when the tree falls.[19]

As in this tale, diverse communities today often wonder if colleges are really on their side. What does it mean to be there "when the tree falls"? What kind of partnerships lead to the kind of trust that's demanded? How can we conceptualize healthy campus-community partnerships as dialogue? This last question is especially relevant here.

Campus-community partnerships, when conceptualized as dialogue, involve campus and community partners who are eager to share a worldview, agree about goals, and have mutual trust and respect. To do this, campus partners must spend time learning about the community context, including the history of the community, community assets, and current concerns. They must also learn about the broader social, political, and economic contexts of the community and be prepared to reevaluate personal prejudices, stereotypes, and biases they may harbor about the community. This calls for prolonged and multifaceted engagement of college partners with the community.

Campus-community partnerships as dialogue also suggest that partners must conduct partnership activities in a manner that is attentive to issues of power and effective communication. Available literature reveals that partnerships are flawed early on when college participants fail to acknowledge that they come into the partnership occupying positions marked by privilege and oppression created by class, educational opportunities, race, language, location, etc. One way to address power differentials is to provide spaces for community partners to name their communities and the problems they face. College partners must trust that community partners can not only name their world, but that they also can come up with solutions to their problems. When community partners are acknowledged as the experts of their world, the partnership is able to devise strategies to tackle daunting social problems. Campus and community dialoguers, in this case, enjoy a horizontal relationship based on trust, mutual respect, and mutually beneficial goals.

A conceptualization of campus-community partnerships as dialogue expects that partners will seek to enhance the organizational capacities of the community partners. As Boyer would argue, institutions of higher learning have a responsibility to improve the less endowed communities. A primary focus of partnering colleges should be to increase the organizational capacities of the community partners with whom they work. This may take the form of professional expertise from faculty, staff, and students, funding, and other forms of material support. Funding is especially critical toward this end. It is also important that control of the funds is shared by institutions.[20] The fact of the matter is like the peasants in Freire's story, many distressed communities already know "how to fell the tree." However, they lack the means to fell it or the capacity to deal with the aftermath of its felling. Without sufficient funds and community control of funds obtained through grants, limited social change can happen. The college can and should take a lead in securing grants with the community partners to support desired social change, but this should be done in a manner that ensures equitable collaboration with communities.

A conceptualization of partnerships as dialogue expects that partners will engage in action for social change. Social change initiatives must be anchored in the concreteness of the world as experienced by community members. Because the reality in most distressed communities is complex and interconnected, activities or projects undertaken must be varied, multifaceted, interdisciplinary, and coordinated. However, the way these activities are carried out is just as important. Freire's notion of praxis is helpful here. Freire defines praxis as reflection and action upon the world in order to transform it. He argues that reflection and action occur "in such radical interaction that if one is sacrificed—even in part—the other immediately suffers."[21] Similarly, in healthy partnerships projects need to reflect this reflexivity. Action by itself, according to Freire, leads to mere "activism," while reflection without action results in "verbalism." Participatory research can help facilitate the social praxis suggested here. Reardon rightly observes that "participatory action research focuses on the information and analytical needs of society's most economically, politically, and socially marginalized groups and communities, and pursues research on issues determined by the leaders of these groups."[22] Because of the multifaceted nature of problems that face distressed communities, action that results from participatory research often leads to further opportunities for more conversation, more research, and more action. When community and campus partners are involved in social praxis, it is likely that their distinct needs will be met. Community partners clarify their focus and generate the data they need to facilitate change. On the campus side, opportunities open up for faculty and students to engage in research, volunteer work, and service-learning opportunities with community partners.

Finally, campus-community partnerships as dialogue are transformational, not transactional. In making the distinction between the two, Enos and Morton note that while efforts based on transactional relationships require little change in the way partners conduct their affairs, partnerships based on transformational relationships can be "dynamic, joint creations in which all the people involved create knowledge, transact power, mix personal and institutional interests, and make meaning."[23] Transformational partnerships allow partners to imagine new ways to act on the world using the resources and assets located in the campus, community, and beyond the two into the broader society through grants and partnerships with other entities. In transformational partnerships, campus and community partners recognize the inherent commonalities and motivations that bind them together toward mutually beneficial goals. They "come to understand that they are a part of the same community, with common problems, common interests, common resources, and common capacity to shape one another in profound ways."[24] They also remain acutely aware of power dynamics that may prevent the desired transformation. Partners seek ways to disrupt the reproduction of power in campus-community relationships in which campuses maintain dominance in multiple ways. The ultimate goal should be to have marginalized communities determine and carry out their own agendas toward social transformation. My observations of the Smith-Hillcrest partnership indicate that transformation through partnership is desirable and possible with enhanced institutionalization.

In sum, a conceptualization of healthy campus-community partnerships as dialogue allows us to highlight a number of important characteristics. Healthy campus-community partnerships flourish when campus and community partners:

- Are eager to share a worldview, agree about goals, and have mutual trust and respect.
- Conduct partnership activities in a collaborative manner that is attentive to issues of power and effective communication.
- Focus their activities around the needs of the community identified by the community.

- Seek to enhance the organizational capacities of the community partners.
- Are attentive to both distinct needs and inherent commonalities in goals and purpose that bind them.
- Are flexible and inclusive of multiple partners to address multifaceted challenges facing communities.
- Are willing to engage in long-term action for social change.

CONCLUSION

In answering the two-pronged question posed at the beginning of this chapter (that is, what factors facilitate the creation of healthy campus-community partnerships and what the characteristics of such relationships are), I have described the Smith-Hillcrest partnership. This is an emerging partnership in which I am a participant observer, and I note six significant features that I believe have laid a strong foundation for a healthy campus-community partnership. I have emphasized that a focus on the campus and community partners and their actions can provide insight into healthy campus-community partnerships, and have used the conceptualization of partnerships as dialogue to bring out this point. I have argued that examining campus-community partnerships as dialogue can provide us with a vocabulary with which to explore further the health of campus-community partnerships. The discussion of partnerships as dialogue can also inform the concept of community-engaged teacher education. In typical teacher education programs, diverse communities are often regarded as sites to be used for familiarizing prospective teachers with issues facing diverse student populations. Rarely do teacher education programs venture beyond the school walls to establish relationships with diverse communities that serve the school. Few, therefore, seek to develop reciprocal relationships with community partners. I have argued in this and preceding chapters that, engaged teacher education programs should seek deeper relationships with diverse communities in their efforts to prepare teachers for diversity. My hope is that as my education colleagues and I continue to work with the Hillcrest schools and CBOs and through a wide-range of community based activities, we will model to our students the notion of community partnerships as dialogue.

NOTES

1. Pseudonyms have been used in place of the real names of schools and the community partners.

2. Kerry J. Strand, Nicholas Cutforth, Randy Stoecker, Sam Marullo, and Patrick Donohue, *Community-Based Research and Higher Education: Principles and Practices* (San Francisco: Jossey-Bass, 2003).

3. Michael Q. Patton, *Quantitative Evaluation and Research Methods* (Thousand Oaks, CA: Sage Publications, 1990).

4. See Ernest L. Boyer, "The Scholarship of Engagement"; "Creating the New American College"; and "The Scholarship of Engagement," San Francisco: Jossey-Bass, 2003.

5. Ernest L. Boyer, "The scholarship of engagement," *Bulletin of the American Academy of Arts and Sciences* 49, no. 7 (1996): 18–33.

6. The Hillcrest Strategic Plan, 1.

7. Lucy Mule, "Elucidating Barriers to Community Engagement: Literacy for a Healthier Community Partnership Project (2005–2007)" (unpublished report).

8. Lucy Mule, "Elucidating Barriers."

9. The Hillcrest Campus Committee Resource Guide, 1

10. Community activism ensured the construction of Torres Elementary and the adjacent Blake Middle School. Torres Elementary was built on an underground passage that served as a street connecting the two sections of Hillcrest that were separated when the city built a highway through the neighborhood in the 1950s. Beginning in 1975, the passage housed Hillcrest's first community center, where regular activities for youth and adults were offered. Over the next five years, however, the center lost funding and organizations that had part of the community moved away. One of the goals of the HCC is to return needed services to Hillcrest.

11. Smith college academic departments represented were Education and Child Study, Psychology, and Exercise and Sport Studies. Also represented was staff from Smith's Office of Educational Outreach.

12. Kerry J. Strand et al., *Community-Based Research and Higher Education*, 29.

13. Meredith Minkler and Nina Wallerstein, eds., *Community-Based Participatory Research for Health* (San Francisco: Jossey-Bass, 2003).

14. See Matthew B. Miles and Michael A. Huberman, *Qualitative Data Analysis* (Thousand Oaks, CA: Sage Publications, 1994); Richard Krueger, *Analyzing and Reporting Focus Group Results* (Thousand Oaks, CA: SAGE Publications, 1998).

15. This study is described in detail in Mule, "Elucidating Barriers to Community Engagement."

16. NIH grant proposal. Smith Office for Educational Outreach.

17. See Robert G. Bringle and Julie Hatcher, "Institutionalization of Service Learning in Higher Education," *Journal of Higher Education* 17, no. 3 (2000): 273–90; "Campus-Community Partnerships: The Terms of Engagement," *Journal of Social Issues* 58, no. 3 (2002): 503–16; Mark Langseth, "Maximizing Impact, Minimizing Harm: Why Service-Learning Must More Fully Integrate Multicultural Education," in *Integrating Service-Learning and Multicultural Education in Colleges and Universities*, ed. Carolyn R. O'Grady (Mahwah, NJ: Lawrence Erlbaum Associates, 2000), 45–71.

18. Paulo Freire, *Pedagogy of the Oppressed* (New York: Continuum, 1970), 77.

19. Peter McLaren and Peter Leonard, *Paulo Freire: A Critical Encounter* (New York, NY: Routledge, 1993), 153.

20. For a critique of the inequalities suffered by communities when funding is secured through the college, see Randy Stoecker, "Challenging Institutional Barriers to Community-Based Research," *Action Research* 6, no. 1 (2008): 49–67.

21. Paulo Freire, *Pedagogy*, 75.

22. Kenneth M. Reardon, "Participatory Action Research as Service Learning," *New Directions for Teaching and Learning* 73 (1998): 57–64.

23. Sandra Enos and Keith Morton, "Developing a Theory and Practice of Campus-Community Partnerships," in *Building Partnerships for Service Learning*, ed. Barbara Jacoby (San Francisco, CA: Jossey-Bass, 2003), 20–41.

24. Sandra Enos and Keith Morton, "Developing a Theory," 20.

5

Community-Based Research as Border Crossing: The Promise of CBR and Barriers to Its Institutionalization in Education

In chapter 1, I emphasized that faculty commitment to community engagement is important in efforts to develop a community-engaged teacher education. In chapters 2 and 3, I stressed that MSL and CBR can connect both education students and faculty with economically disadvantaged and culturally diverse communities in ways that are more enduring when compared to CFEs with a lesser community-engagement focus. I also noted the paucity in the literature of options available to education faculty and students leading toward a deeper engagement with communities through CBR. In this chapter I focus on issues related to CBR in education and explore the concept of "border crossing CBR." I emphasize its usefulness in fostering linkages between college and community, expanding knowledge about communities, and transforming pedagogical practices and outcomes. In the second section, I use a personal border crossing experience to discuss four options that education faculty can use to meaningfully infuse CBR into teacher education programs. I also outline some of the barriers that may hinder the institutionalization of border crossing CBR in education, and I conclude the chapter with a discussion on how community-engaged programs in small liberal arts colleges can institutionalize this approach.

THE PROMISE OF BORDER CROSSING CBR IN EDUCATION

The concept of border crossing CBR as used in this chapter draws from two distinct concepts—CBR and border crossing—both of which are

gaining prominence in community-based learning and education literature. Although the concept of CBR is contested, I prefer to use definitions
that emphasize a focus on collaborative research *with* marginalized communities toward social change. One such definition is offered by Strand
et al.:

> CBR is a partnership of students, faculty, and community members who col-
> laboratively engage in research with the purpose of solving a pressing com-
> munity problem or affecting social change. . . . In every case, the community
> consists of people who are oppressed, powerless, economically deprived, or
> disenfranchised—that is, who are disadvantaged by existing social, political,
> or economic arrangements.[1]

This definition draws from the notion of community-based participatory
research (CBPR), which is "an orientation or approach to research that
favors equitable relationships between researchers and community members through collaboration in all phases of the research process."[2] While
collaborative community problem-solving identified in this definition is
an important goal, I posit that it need not be the only goal. Equally important for education faculty is the goal of using CBR/CBPR as a strategy for
preparing students to become effective teachers—and to be social change
agents within their role as educators—in these or similar communities. I
find that the concept of border crossing CBR captures the type of engagement with communities implied by these definitions.

The concept of border crossing in education is mainly associated with
the work of Henry Giroux, a leading theorist who has gained prominence within and outside of the field of education. Urging his readers to
consider border crossing as a political and heuristic metaphor, Giroux
also highlights its strength as a way of thinking about faculty's work as
educators:

> The concept of border crossing not only critiques those borders that confine
> experience and limit the politics of crossing diverse geographical, social,
> cultural, economic, and political borders, it also calls for new ways to forge a
> public pedagogy capable of connecting the local and the global, the economic
> sphere and cultural politics, as well as public and higher education and the
> pressing social demands of the larger society.[3]

Informed by various theoretical discourses including feminism, critical
pedagogy, and postcolonial theory, Giroux's concept of border crossing
calls for an involvement with diverse communities that challenges and
transforms boundaries that have traditionally separated institutions of
higher education from neighboring communities. When applied to CBR,

the concept of border crossing helps to clarify the promise of the CBR model in engaging education faculty and students in diverse communities.

Border crossing in its literal sense is not a new phenomenon for teacher educators. Many education professors already cross borders into the K–12 schools with which they work closely in preparing teachers. University/college-school partnership models such as the professional development school (PDS) have been quite successful in facilitating border crossing to K–12 schools.[4] However, faculty border crossings that go beyond school walls into communities are less widespread. They are even less common when the communities in question are poor and of color.[5] The CBR model suggests crossing into communities that involves more than the literal sense of the word and a charity or service level of engagement. Three benefits engendered by the border crossing CBR model make it attractive as a strategy for preparing future teachers for diversity. First, the border crossing CBR model recognizes the need to build bridges with communities toward a mutual and reciprocal relationship. Second, it embraces the notion of expanded knowledge, acknowledging that prospective teachers benefit from knowledge generated within the community. Third, it allows for the enactment of what I will refer to as "community-engaged pedagogy." The following discussion elaborates on each of these areas.

Building Bridges with Communities

In general, as many have noted, schools, colleges, and departments of education (SCDEs) have been isolationist toward neighboring communities. Melnick and Zeichner discuss the "cultural insularity" that both causes and results from this stance,[6] and Giroux sees this isolation as indicative of the abandonment of civic responsibility by SCDEs.[7] Shirley and colleagues underscore the need to address the distance between SCDEs and communities when they urge preservice teacher education reform efforts to "overcome the cultural encapsulation of higher education faculty from urban diversity that in many ways has undermined not only the efficacy but also the democratic promise of teacher education in a multicultural society."[8] Border crossing CBR offers an opportunity for SCDEs to bridge with communities. In thinking about building bridges through CBR, Strand et al. emphasize the need to pursue relationships with grassroots community-based organizations (CBOs) and/or other agencies serving the community, as long they do not "disempower community members" and have "demonstrated a real commitment to their constituent communities."[9] In working with CBOs or similar agencies through CBR, faculty can build bridges to minimize the distance between communities and institutions of higher learning. They can, in the words of Giroux, "come into communities with their resources and possibilities so that [they] can begin to create borderlands of dialogue and struggles."[10]

Expanded Knowledge about Communities

A second benefit underlying border crossing CBR is the growing understanding that all knowledge does not reside on university or college campuses, and that communities and their people are valid sources of locally derived practical knowledge that is critically needed in order to revitalize teaching practices and school reform. Popular concepts such as "funds of knowledge," "bridging cultures," "community teachers," and "public intellectuals" all speak to this perspective. Giroux's use of the concept of public intellectual is especially persuasive in its emphasis on the need for educators in institutions of higher education to seek deeper engagement with communities for knowledge production. The term public intellectuals is broad and encompasses people involved with education work, including those residing outside of educational institutions—that is, people in communities who provide "the moral, political, and pedagogical leadership for those groups which take as their starting point the transformative critique of the conditions of oppression."[11] Giroux urges educators within educational institutions to expand their notions of education and pedagogy and to regard themselves as cultural workers and as part of a larger system of public intellectuals, some of whom reside in communities. Giroux further urges that the borders separating academics and public intellectuals in communities should be broken around different kinds of local projects.[12]

Border crossing CBR is one such project that provides opportunities for education faculty and students to work collaboratively with community partners, while allowing both faculty and college students to gain deeper insights into the community and to participate in the process of social transformation. Education faculty who cross borders through CBR see value in the practical knowledge residing in community partners and contexts, and consider both to be powerful resources in the education of future teachers. They also see communities as sites in which they can integrate their teaching, research, and service goals. Through CBR faculty and students get an opportunity to expand their knowledge about communities and the social contexts of education and pedagogy. Communities benefit from knowledge developed through collaborative research, which is likely to be more relevant than imported knowledge and theories constructed away from their lived reality.

Community-Engaged Pedagogy

Some of the most attractive aspects of the border crossing CBR model that I will explore here are its (1) potential to transform traditional forms of teaching based on the transmission model, (2) ability to develop in college students the necessary skills to work *with* rather than *for* communities,[13] (3) capacity to develop self and social critique in future teachers, and (4) focus on participation in the process of social change. These four are key features of what I refer to here as community-engaged pedagogy.

In terms of transforming pedagogy on campus, faculty teaching CBR courses take seriously the invitation to their students to cross the borders of meanings, and put theory into practice. Theirs is a perpetuation of the quest to unify theory and practice that is advocated by such influential thinkers as John Dewey and Paulo Freire, who argue that "knowledge is a participatory, transactional, and reflective act."[14] Rather than a "banking" model of knowledge production (as expressed by Freire),[15] they see education as a collaborative project between professors and students in which knowledge is constructed rather than simply received. In CBR courses, this project will include community-based partners, as well.

Beyond adopting more collaborative and participatory models in their pedagogy through CBR, an important goal of CBR pedagogues is to guide their college students to develop a language in which they speak *with* rather than *for* the communities, and engage in a discourse that allows them to participate in projects that, to use Giroux's words, "utilize human differences to expand the potential of human life and democratic possibilities."[16] Instead of the traditional approach where academia designs and implements projects *for* the community, CBR allows for a shared discourse in which academia works collaboratively *with* the community to respond to community needs and concerns. Buck and Sylvester explain how preservice teachers' gendered, classed, and racialized experiences may interfere with their ability to work *with* communities.[17] Many scholars also have critiqued the noblesse oblige perspective which tends to inform many community-based learning experiences.[18] CBR's emphasis on a deep involvement with community members within their contexts may lead students to reexamine personal biases and encourage them to adopt a community assets perspective. It also embraces flexibility in community and college partners in the roles of expert, teacher, learner, and agent of social change. CBR pedagogues model to students fluidity among these roles.

The third emphasis in the CBR pedagogy is on the goal for both faculty and students to develop self and social awareness and critique. Faculty using the CBR model are likely to be self-critical, at classroom and institutional levels, about their purposes, goals, and actions, as well as ways these allow or hinder the process of developing future teachers for diversity. CBR mirrors other pedagogical models for preservice teachers that have emphasized gaining a critical self and social awareness, developing a language of critique, and adopting a classroom-based pedagogy reflecting these understandings. Examples include "equity pedagogy," "justice pedagogy," "culturally responsive pedagogy," "critical pedagogy," and "border pedagogy." All these models have in common a commitment to teaching for social justice. According to Darling-Hammond:

> Learning to teach for social justice is a lifelong undertaking. It involves coming to understand oneself in relation to others; examining how society constructs privilege and inequality and how this affects one's own opportunities as well as those of different people; exploring the experiences of others and appreciating how those inform their world views, perspectives, and opportunities; and evaluating how schools and classrooms operate and can be structured to value diverse human experiences and to enable learning for all students.[19]

Through their engagement with communities through CBR, college students may gain the self and social awareness to which Darling-Hammond refers. When their experience is coupled with appropriate course readings and reflection, they may gain a theoretical grasp of ways in which student learning in schools "is bound within larger contextual, social, historical, political, and ideological frameworks that affect students' lives."[20] For instance, through combining carefully selected theoretical material with their CBR experience, preservice teachers may gain a deeper understanding of how enduring educational challenges in many marginalized communities—such as achievement gap, low graduation and high dropout rates, tracking, unequal educational funding, high-stakes testing—are inextricably related to wider social and systemic structures.

Finally, CBR enables community-engaged pedagogy when involvement in it leads to commitment to social change. For instance, through involvement in CBR, future teachers may begin to develop strategies that could allow them to engage in teaching for social justice; that is, in ways that confront social power mapping and ways that schools function to reproduce the status quo. Some research indicates that preservice teachers who acquire these strategies during their college education are likely to engage in teaching for social justice in their school classrooms.[21]

The three areas discussed above—building bridges with communities through enduring and reciprocal partnerships, embracing expanded knowledge by participating in collaborative production of knowledge, and engaging in community-oriented pedagogy—point to key elements of border crossing CBR in education. In sum, border crossing CBR in education has the following four key principles:

- *Based on inclusive, collaborative, and reciprocal college-community partnerships.* CBR flourishes in a bilateral partnership context involving community-based and college-based partners. In education, trilateral partnerships are desirable as they also include school-based partners. It is important to note that only those school-based partners who are committed to empowering communities would be appropriate. In such cases, CBR supports other theories of partnerships, such as Epstein's theory of overlapping spheres of influence, which asserts that "[K–12] students succeed at higher levels when home, school, and [institutions of higher education] work together to support students' learning and development."[22] Reciprocity, clear communication, and respect are critical in both bilateral and trilateral partnerships.
- *Embraces multiple sources of knowledge.* Education faculty and students see communities as valid sources and creators of knowledge. Establishing relationships with individuals leading community-based organizations and/or directly with families is key to accessing knowledge residing in communities. Reciprocal relationships allow college partners access to communities' "funds of knowledge" and allow communities to benefit from increased research capacities.
- *Promotes a pedagogy based on self and social critique.* Border crossing CBR encourages an examination of privileges accrued from an individual's membership in socially constructed categories (including race, ethnicity, class, and language), and how these influence one's view of the "other." It also emphasizes a comprehensive understanding of social problems, including educational ones, as being inextricably bound within broader social structures. These links are examined within their sociocultural and historical specificity. An understanding of this structural embeddedness is critical, and action resulting from CBR must reflect this understanding.
- *Focused on community action and social change.* Border crossing CBR combines participatory and empowerment research traditions to seek solutions to enduring problems affecting the community. Rather than focusing only on empowerment for a few individuals, action resulting from border crossing CBR must target the long-term and comprehensive well-being of the community; what Murrell calls "the community development agenda."[23]

These principles of border crossing CBR provide general guidelines for contemplating CBR in education. In their own contexts, teacher educators have struggled with the challenges of integrating community-based learning into their practice. In the following section I revisit a personal border crossing CBR experience (detailed in chapter 4) to underline the CBR options available in education. Next I outline some of the barriers that may hinder the institutionalization of border crossing CBR in education, and I end the chapter with some reflections on what it takes to institutionalize this approach in education.

PERSONAL NARRATIVE OF BORDER CROSSING THROUGH CBR: MINDING THE STUDENT AND ADOPTING THE OPTIONS APPROACH

In chapter 4 I offered a personal narrative of a border crossing through a community-based participatory research project, "Elucidating Barriers to Literacy Study." I return to that narrative here for three reasons. First, to examine the extent to which the CBR project reflected some of the key components of border crossing CBR outlined in the previous section. Second, to imagine better ways to involve education students in CBR opportunities in contexts akin to the Hillcrest community. Third, to emphasize the need for faculty to consider what I call the "options approach" in infusing CBR in education.

To recap, the "Elucidating Barriers to Literacy Study" was a community-based participatory research project that took place over a period of one year and involved community–based, school-based, and college-based partners. The trilateral nature of the partnership that supported the study was inspired by the visionary school principal of Torres Elementary, Julio Ortiz. Although facing intense pressure to raise his school's high stakes test scores, Ortiz persisted in prioritizing strategies that would address the complex social and educational challenges that confront the Hillcrest community. A three-year NIH grant facilitated the development of a Hillcrest-Smith college-community partnership with a focus on improving the long-term well-being of the community, not just bolstering the test results of grade students.

The goals of the partnership emphasized a focus on researching and addressing Hillcrest community needs around literacy. In this sense, the partnership reflected a participatory research model that emphasizes research, education, and action, as well as community empowerment, where community partners gain mastery of their affairs.[24] Research questions and data collection tools (a survey and focus groups) were jointly developed by college, community, and school partners. Although I and two Smith students were responsible for analyzing data and producing a report, we sought feedback from other partners at every step of this process. It was hoped that the study would provide direction to the nature of the community family literacy center that would effectively serve the needs of families, the school, and other community residents. I have discussed this study elsewhere in detail including research questions, methodology used, and findings.[25] In chapter 4, I highlighted aspects of the research project that evoke some of the tenets of border crossing CBR. The "Elucidating Barriers to Literacy Study" was formulated within an inclusive and collaborative partnership, focused on a community-identified problem, and sought to address long-term well-being of the community through developing a framework for addressing barriers to literacy for all. However, I also noted the minimal involvement of one key participant—the college students.

From the description of this CBR project (see details in chapter 4) it is clear that students were only minimally involved in the research activities of this grassroots organization. For instance, no students were involved in choosing the focus of the research, research design and method, or data collection. Two Smith education students helped with transcription, translation, management, and analyses of the data. One student helped prepare the drafts and final report submitted to community partners. Yet this project, for all its inability to involve students more meaningfully, demonstrated for me the need to consider integration of border crossing CBR in education. Inclusion of college students in CBR strengthens the academic justification for continued partnership with Hillcrest, which is needed to garner the institutional support to sustain college-community partnerships.

INFUSING BORDER CROSSING CBR:
THE OPTIONS APPROACH

In this section, I use hypothetical education courses to outline CBR options that are available to faculty. Agreeing with Strand et al.'s observation that faculty need flexibility in choosing CBR alternatives that work for their courses, I outline four possibilities for infusing CBR in education: CBR as an optional component of the course, CBR as methodology, CBR as internship / independent study, and CBR as classroom-based pedagogy. In examining these options, I prefer to think in terms of curricular focus rather than course name or level. As practiced, each of the CBR options will vary in terms of number of students involved, individual versus group emphasis, optional or required participation, nature of assignments, theoretical readings, time commitment in communities, level of structured reflection, type and number of CBOs involved, nature of partnership with CBOs, and level of supervision required. These factors will also influence the roles of the faculty, students, and community partners, as well as the targeted goals of the CBR experience for each partner.

CBR as an Optional Component of the Course

CBR as an optional component of a course would be most commonly used in beginning- and intermediate-level education courses. These courses would attract a wide range of students who differ in skill levels, motivation, exposure, and confidence. The goal of these courses would be to allow students to make contributions to surrounding communities while enhancing academic and personal skills. Courses within this option would engage all students in service-learning projects—such as tutoring and mentoring K–12 students and assisting in local centers, e.g., shelters, soup kitchens, health agencies, sports programs, public libraries, and adult education and ESL programs—but keep CBR available only to students who are capable, willing, and can invest the time needed. CBR involvement at this level should be kept to simple projects; for example, working with CBOs to identify grant sources and write grants, collecting oral histories of residents, researching and compiling databases of community assets and services, designing and administering simple surveys, offering support to and evaluating short-term projects, and evaluating long-term CBO-run programs. The latent disadvantage to this approach, in addition to the organizational challenges it presents for the professor, is that CBR students are likely to feel disconnected from the rest of the class.

CBR as Methodology

The focus of CBR as self-contained methodology courses would be to enhance CBOs' capacity for research, increase students' knowledge about community, and develop student knowledge about research. Professors would carefully select a number of community-based research projects that are doable within the time available in the course. The projects would be based on issues identified as important by community partners. The instructor and community partners would set realistic goals for student research and anticipate challenges that students are likely to encounter— and ways to deal with them. The projects would be completed by students in groups and would involve working collaboratively with community partners and faculty at each step—developing research questions, developing data collection tools, analyzing data, and preparing a report. In a research methodology course such as this, student involvement would be mandatory. In each step, students would be required to meet with community partners and simultaneously keep abreast of course readings on research broadly (and CBR specifically), as well on the specific social issue upon which they are focusing. Students would be provided with the scaffolding and supervision they need to complete projects, write reports, and present them on campus and in communities. The Elucidating Barriers to Literacy Study described in chapter 4 would have fallen into this category, if it had been tied in with an education research course.

CBR as Internship

This option would ideally be undertaken by education students who would have had prior exposure to the community and would have developed a certain level of comfort or relationship with a particular CBO. Students, for example, would have completed prior pre-practicum, tutoring, or other forms of service-learning and developed an interest in deepening their relationship with community through research. At the point of taking up a research-focused internship, students would have enough time, knowledge of community, faculty support, academic skills, and confidence needed to engage in sustained research within a community. There are many reasons why students may engage in CBR internships with CBOs. More colleges are now offering some financial support to students when they intern with CBOs. At Smith College, for instance, students can spend 220 hours working in a community organization of their choice and receive a stipend through the Praxis program. Prolonged engagement with communities provides an opportunity for students to engage in CBR. Work completed during an internship may also carry academic credit if it is directed by faculty. Since the completion of the Elucidating Barriers to Literacy Study community project, the partners and I have had conversations on how to better make use of this option to connect Smith education students to the research needs in the Hillcrest community.

CBR as Independent Study

CBR as independent study would be credit-bearing and would be completed during the regular school year. It could be turned into a senior thesis in education. Thus, it would involve readings and faculty mentoring that would enhance student research skills and deepen knowledge about community and the research topic. For instance, one of the students who assisted in the data analyses and writing of the report in the Elucidating Barriers to Literacy Study earned credit for this work and for a related independent study research paper she wrote and presented at a regional education conference. Independent research studies completed by students are often helpful in community advocacy efforts.

CBR as Classroom Pedagogy

This option would be possible when student teachers have been strategically placed with K–12 teachers who integrate CBR in their teaching.

The work of such teachers is widely documented.[26] The student teacher role would involve working with the mentor teacher or individually to collaborate with community partners in developing, guiding, and supervising students in research projects involving issues of importance to the community. The goal would be to enhance the student teacher's practice based on the principles of social justice / culturally responsive pedagogy and to build bridges with families and communities. Besides increasing their academic skills, K–12 students would be empowered through research to participate in community development and social change, and communities benefit from deeper youth engagement with community issues.

The options model detailed in this section offers a flexible approach to the integration of CBR in education.

OF THE BARRIERS TO THE INSTITUTIONALIZATION OF BORDER CROSSING CBR IN EDUCATION

It is obvious that a certain amount of institutionalization is needed to facilitate border crossing CBR work in education. However, it is important to be fully cognizant of the many barriers that can stand in the way of institutionalization of CBR in education. Barriers to the institutionalization of border crossing CBR are wide-ranging, but can be broadly categorized into four broad areas: practical / logistical; pedagogical; departmental/ institutional; and ideological / political.[27] Following an outline of these barriers is a discussion of what it takes to institutionalize the border crossing CBR approach in education.

The Practical/Logistical Barriers

These barriers speak to the time and other resources required to organize a border crossing CBR course. First, it takes faculty time to be introduced to, and then develop strong relationships with, communities. In border crossing CBR, with its emphasis on partnership and collaboration among partners, it is expected that quality relationships may take longer to develop when compared to less intense college-community interactions. Second, whether CBR constitutes an entire course or just part of it, faculty end up dedicating more time that they would in a regular course. The demands on faculty time will further increase depending on students' level of readiness, type of partnership with community sites and the amount of research supervision they can offer, and the amount of support available from the institution to facilitate logistics, such as transportation. When enough time and relevant support (including funding, staff to coordinate students, and an appropriate reward system) are in place, the practical barriers are significantly lessened.

The Pedagogical Barriers

These barriers reveal the complexity of integrating border crossing CBR in regular courses in education. It is commonly agreed that for most professors, their interest in working with communities makes sense when it is properly integrated into courses they commonly teach.[28] However, for this integration to occur several conditions need to be in place including (1) explicitly relating community-based work to course goals, class format, and student evaluation, (2) "walking the talk," where professors work in communities alongside their students, (3) prolonged engagement with community sites, and (4) recognition of the role of community members as co-researchers and co-educators. These conditions contain assumptions that may be contrary to the prevailing beliefs and practices associated with college-level teaching. Many college courses last one semester, the focus is on rigor in engaging disciplinary content knowledge, and—despite the reform talk—teaching is often seen as an activity involving one instructor and a roomful of students, based on the transmission model (where instructors transfer established knowledge to students). This model requires that a sufficient knowledge distance between the professor and students and/or the community is acknowledged and maintained. Anything short of that is likely to be viewed with suspicion as "less than." Moreover, the evaluation of students in many college courses is expected to reflect these expectations. Institution-wide course evaluations in which students provide feedback on the course and the professor also reflect these assumptions.

The Departmental/Institutional Barriers

Many departments of education are ill-prepared to accommodate border crossing CBR. Although calls to academia (citing pedagogical value and civic responsibility) to participate meaningfully in communities have increased since the 1980s, action suggesting a radical shift from "business as usual" is rare in most education departments.[29] Department-specific factors may stymie efforts to infuse CBR in education. First, rarely do education departments have spaces to which communities can come to communicate their research needs. Usually, crossings into the community are lonely and made by individual faculty members (rather than departments), often fueled by their need to provide rich learning opportunities for their students rather than to engage meaningfully with communities' core concerns. Course structure dictates that these engagements are semester-long and that community engagement becomes one component of the course rather than the central focus of the course. Departmental ethos is such that work completed by either students or faculty while in communities is hardly ever made public, and when it is, it's never in ways that invite a deepened and sustained dialogue on relevant communities with either or both college and community members. To be fair, education departments are often inundated by commitments to K–12 schools and resist the temptation to spread resources too thinly. Faculty committed to CBR involving non-school contexts may be misconstrued to be insensitive to this concern, especially when resources are particularly scarce.

Another threat to institutionalization of border crossing CBR in education relates to broader challenges that faculty in education and across the disciplines face in justifying CBR as credible scholarship in academia. Researchers have argued for high integration in which the research, teaching, and community service roles of the faculty are harmonized and this value is reflected in the evaluative process.[30] A lack of adequate mechanisms to address this scholarship barrier may contribute to a lack of institutionalization of border crossing CBR in education, as many faculty are reluctant to take the risk that comes with breaking from traditional boundaries of scholarship. Furthermore, border crossing CBR requires a reconceptualization of taken-for-granted notions of knowledge ownership and control of research funding. As Randy Stoecker has argued, traditional forms of research in diverse communities have reinforced higher education's power to "maintain control over knowledge production." Higher education traditions also "[limit] what can be considered 'legitimate' research, and restrict the uses to which funding can be put."[31] Faculty working in border crossing CBR are expected to relinquish their power over knowledge ownership and funding and to work collaboratively and equitably with community members in these two areas. This role adjustment may add to faculty reluctance to participate in border crossing CBR, especially if they are operating within traditional institutions.

The Ideological/Political Barriers

This category of barriers arises from a point made earlier, that border crossing CBR is both a pedagogical and a political model. While being political in itself is not problematic, we live, as Butin (referencing Westheimer and Kahne) has observed, in an environment where the "fundamentally distinctive models of what it means to be a citizen . . . are all too easily transposed into, and associated with, left- and right-wing agendas and ideologies."[32] It follows that CBR that appears to advocate for a deep understanding of and response to the felt needs of the community and change toward social justice is likely to be viewed with suspicion, especially if the institutional stance is more conservative, "objective," or "professional." The border crossing stance, in contrast, sees both students and faculty as cultural workers and partners working closely with a network of groups of people in communities toward social action and transformation, with objectives of a stronger democracy and/or learning to teach for social justice.[33] Mutual goals, issues, and needs in the community, rather than course structures on campus, drive border crossing CBR courses. In this sense, CBR is more likely than the more conservative forms of field-based learning to be meshed in left/right political agendas and conflicts that result. Westheimer explains how these wars have intensified and become more pronounced in the K–16 landscape since September 2001.[34] Many teacher educators, while political, want to keep away from politics and therefore avoid border crossing CBR.

STRATEGIES FOR INSTITUTIONALIZING BORDER CROSSING CBR IN EDUCATION

Despite the barriers outlined above, I have argued elsewhere in this book that developing deep relationships with marginalized communities is not only desirable but urgent in teacher education programs committed to the process and goal of preparing effective teachers for America's diverse classrooms. Institutionalization is therefore a key issue that preservice teacher education programs would need to address. This section outlines three strategies for institutionalizing border crossing CBR in education and discusses why they are likely to work in liberal arts college contexts: (1) development of specific courses and careful sequencing of existing courses, (2) establishment of collaborative and reciprocal partnerships with selected CBOs, and (3) collaboration with college-wide interdisciplinary structures or centers.

CBR-Focused Courses

The first strategy for institutionalizing border crossing CBR involves a strategic rethinking of course offerings. Teacher education programs in liberal arts colleges have sought to increase their students' knowledge of marginalized communities through the inclusion of special courses and integrating CFEs in education courses. An exhaustive discussion on integrating CFEs in education was provided in chapter 2, and the importance of departmental ownership emphasized. The commitment by the department to "own" CBR is especially critical. With regard to CBR this ownership can be done in a number of ways, including setting up a fund to support community partners to provide guest lecturers in education courses, developing department-owned (rather than individual faculty-owned) long-term projects that are run in collaboration with communities and can provide research opportunities for many students and faculty, and providing resource rooms where all CBR reports are housed and made available to college and community members. This level of visibility of departmental ownership of CBR can in turn influence the college-level commitment to community-based research for both faculty and students.

Partnerships with CBOs

Forming collaborative and reciprocal partnerships with selected CBOs is a way to enhance the community-based research capacity of teacher education. Many critics of current reforms in preservice teacher education fault most initiatives for not developing in preservice teachers a deep relationship with and/or understanding of communities that serve the schools in which they teach. Involving preservice teachers in border crossing CBR may deepen their knowledge of communities, thus increasing their competence as future teachers. Such involvement also helps in addressing community-identified needs. Some features of liberal arts colleges may make it possible, at least in theory, to seek partnerships with CBOs in disenfranchised communities. Some of these were outlined in chapter 1. These strengths notwithstanding, departments of education in liberal arts colleges are faced with challenges related to their size that may dim their attractiveness to communities. An obvious downside to their size is that they may lack the mechanisms and capacities that would allow them to (1) meet local manpower needs that often overwhelm communities (e.g., teacher education programs should ideally work closely with marginalized communities to develop a cadre of teachers from those communities for community schools), (2) garner significant grants *with* diverse communities to support community development initiatives, and (3) provide faculty and students with the training that is required to successfully engage in border crossing CBR. Furthermore, the "advocacy" or "political activism" form of involvement with communities has its share of critics in education, many of whom work hard to keep departments from committing to the social justice teacher education reform agenda.

Collaboration with College-Wide
Interdisciplinary Structures or Centers

Education departments are seen as exemplars in many campuses of partnerships with schools.[35] Expanding their purview to include border crossing CBR will enhance this already established superiority and leadership. In their efforts to institutionalize border crossing CBR, education departments should partner with campus-wide structures or interdisciplinary centers, especially those that promote community engagement for social change. As noted in chapter 1, such centers function to help students and faculty connect to the research and technical needs of community organizations, and often offer logistical support and funding needed to complete CBR. When education departments work closely with centers such as these, they benefit from the availability of additional college resources (transportation, community orientation, research coordination, funding, research training, and general oversight). Such linkages can serve to institutionalize CBR at both departmental and college-wide levels.

CONCLUSION

Border crossing CBR can help strengthen mutually beneficial partnerships between college (faculty and students) and community partners. I argue in this chapter that such partnerships are critical to teacher education reform efforts, as they serve as a bridge between college and community, help generate important knowledge about communities, and allow for the enactment of community-oriented pedagogies needed to prepare teachers for diversity. However, institutionalizing border crossing CBR is daunting and requires a great deal of commitment to (and creativity in) addressing barriers—practical / logistical, pedagogical, institutional / departmental, and ideological / political—that may impede the process. Despite these barriers, it is important to emphasize that education departments in liberal arts colleges also enjoy some strengths that would support the institutionalization of border crossing CBR. Ultimately, a commitment to community engagement in general, and border crossing CBR specifically, can facilitate the process of preparing effective future teachers for America's diverse classrooms.

NOTES

1. Kerry J. Strand, Nicholas Cutforth, Randy Stoecker, Sam Marullo, and Patrick Donohue, *Community-Based Research and Higher Education: Principles and Practices* (San Francisco: Jossey-Bass, 2003), 3.

2. Anya Y. Spector, "Book Review: Community-Based Participatory Research for Health: From Process to Outcomes," *Health Promotion Practice* 10, no. 3 (July 2009): 317; Meredith Minkler and Nina Wallerstein, eds., *Community-Based Participatory Research for Health*, 2nd ed. (San Francisco: Jossey-Bass, 2008); Carol R. Horowitz, Mimsie Robinson, and Sarena Seifer, "Community-Based Participatory Research's Journey from Margins to Mainstream: Are Researchers Prepared?" *Circulation* 119 (2009): 2633–42.

3. Henry Giroux, *Border Crossings: Cultural Workers and the Politics of Education* (New York: Routledge, 2005).

4. See Linda Darling-Hammond, *Professional Development Schools: Schools for Developing a Profession* (New York: Teachers College Press, 1994); Ismat Abdal-Haqq, *Professional Development Schools: Weighing the Evidence* (Thousand Oaks, CA: Corwin Press, 1998); Lee Teitel, *The Professional Development Schools Handbook: Starting, Sustaining, and Assessing Partnerships That Improve Student Learning* (Thousand Oaks, CA: Corwin Press, 2003).

5. Lenore Reilly Carlisle, Bailey W. Jackson, and Allison George, "Principles of Social Justice Education: The Social Justice Education in Schools Project," *Equity & Excellence in Education* 39 (2006): 55–64; Peter C. Murrell, *The Community Teacher: A New Framework for Effective Urban Teaching* (New York: Teachers College Press, 2001); Mari Koerner and Najwa Abdul-Tawwab, "Using Community as a Resource for Teacher Education: A Case Study," *Equity & Excellence in Education* 39 (2006): 37–46.

6. Susan L. Melnick and Kenneth M. Zeichner, "Teacher Education's Responsibility to Address Diversity Issues: Enhancing Institutional Capacity," in *Preparing Teachers for Cultural Diversity*, ed. Joyce E. King, Etta R. Hollins, and Warren C. Hayman (New York: Teachers College Press, 1997).

7. Henry Giroux, *Border Crossings*.

8. Dennis Shirley, Afra Hersi, Elizabeth MacDonald, Maria Sanchez, Connie Scandone, Charles Skidmore, Patrick Tutwiler, "Bringing the Community Back in: Change, Accommodation, and Contestation in a School University Partnership," *Equity & Excellence in Education* 39 (2006): 27–36.

9. Kerry J. Strand et al., *Community-Based Research and Higher Education*, 74.

10. Henry Giroux, *Border Crossings*, 135.

11. Henry Giroux, *Teachers as Intellectuals: Toward a Critical Pedagogy of Learning* (Westport, CT: Bergin & Garvey Publishers, Inc., 1988), 153.

12. Henry Giroux, *Border Crossings*, 135.

13. Kelly Ward and Lisa Wolf-Wendel, "Community-Centered Service Learning: Moving from Doing for to Doing With," *American Behavioral Scientist* 43, no. 5 (2000): 767–80.

14. See Dan W. Butin, "Disciplining Service Learning: Institutionalization and the Case for Community Studies," *International Journal of Teaching and Learning in Higher Education* 18, no. 1 (2006): 58.

15. See Paulo Freire, "Teachers as Cultural Workers: Letters to Those Who Dare Teach" (Boulder: Westview Press, 1998).

16. Henry Giroux, *Border Crossings*, 26.

17. Patricia Buck and Paul Skilton Sylvester, "Preservice Teachers Enter Urban Communities: Coupling Funds of Knowledge Research and Critical Pedagogy in Teacher Education," in *Funds of Knowledge: Theorizing Practices in Households, Communities, and Classrooms*, ed. Norma Gonzáles, Luis C. Moll, and Cathy Amanti (Mahwah, NJ: Lawrence Erlbaum Associates, Publishers, 2005).

18. Anonymous reviewer. See also Marilynne Boyle-Baise, "Community Service-Learning for Multicultural Education: An Exploratory Study with Preservice Teachers," *Equity & Excellence of Education*, 31 (1998): 52–60; Marilynne Boyle-

Baise and Christine Sleeter, "Community-Based Service Learning for Multicultural Teacher Education," *Educational Foundations* 14 (2000): 33–50.

19. Linda Darling-Hammond, "Educating a Profession for Equitable Practice," in *Learning to Teach for Social Justice*, ed. Linda Darling-Hammond, J. Jennifer French, and Silvia Paloma Garcia-Lopez (New York: Teachers College, Columbia University, 2002), 210–12.

20. Norma González, Luis C. Moll, and Cathy Amanti, eds., *Funds of Knowledge: Theorizing Practices in Households, Communities, and Classrooms* (Mahwah, NJ: Lawrence Erlbaum Associates, Inc., Publishers, 2005), ix.

21. Sondra Cuban and Jeffrey B. Anderson, "Where's the Justice in Service-Learning? Institutionalizing Service-Learning from a Social Justice Perspective at a Jesuit University," *Equity & Excellence in Education* 40, no. 2 (2007): 144–55; Linda Darling-Hammond, "Educating a Profession"; Lisa Smulyan, "'The Power of a Teacher': Teacher Education for Social Justice," in *Taking Teaching Seriously: How Liberal Arts Colleges Prepare Teachers to Meet Today's Educational Challenges*, ed. Christopher Bjork, D. Kay Johnston, and Heidi Ross (Boulder, CO: Paradigm Publishers, 2007), 80–99.

22. Joyce L. Epstein and Mavis Sanders, "Prospects for Change: Preparing Educators for School, Family, and Community Partnerships," *Peabody Journal of Education* 81, no. 2 (2006): 81–120.

23. Peter C. Murrell, *The Community Teacher*, 31.

24. See Nina Wallerstein and Bonnie Duran, "The Conceptual, Historical, and Practice Roots of Community-Based Participatory Research and Related Participatory Traditions," in *Community-Based Participatory Research for Health*, ed. Minkler and Nina Wallerstein (San Francisco: Jossey-Bass, 2003), 27–52; Kysa Nygreen, Soo Ah Kwon, and Patricia Sanchez, "Urban Youth Building Community: Social Change and Participatory Research in Schools, Homes, and Community-Based Organizations," *Journal of Community Practice* 14, nos. 1 and 2 (September 2006): 107–23.

25. Lucy Mule, "Elucidating Barriers to Community Engagement: Literacy for a Healthier Community Partnership Project (2005–2007)" (unpublished report).

26. See Mary Cowhey, *Black Ants and Buddhists: Thinking and Teaching Differently in Primary Grades* (Portland, ME: Stenhouse Publishers, 2006); Norma González, Luis C. Moll, and Cathy Amanti, eds., *Funds of Knowledge: Theorizing Practices in Households, Communities, and Classrooms* (Mahwah, NJ: L. Erlbaum Associates, 2005); Rahima C. Wade, "Service-Learning for Social Justice in the Elementary Classroom: Can We Get There from Here?" *Equity & Excellence in Education* 40 (2007): 156–65; Elise Trumbull, Carrie Rothstein-Fisch, Patricia M Greenfield, and Blanca Quiroz, *Bridging Cultures between Home and School: A Guide for Teachers* (Mahwah, NJ: Lawrence Erlbaum Associates, 2001).

27. Some of the categories have been generated following the work of Butin, who has explored limits of service-learning at the college level. See Dan W. Butin, "The Limits of Service-Learning in Higher Education," *The Review of Higher Education* 29, no. 4 (2006): 473–98.

28. See for example, Dan W. Butin, "Of What Use Is It? Multiple Conceptualizations of Service Learning within Education," *Teachers College Record* 105, no.

9 (2003): 1674–92; Carolyn R. O'Grady, ed., *Integrating Service-Learning and Multicultural Education in Colleges and Universities* (Mahwah, NJ: Lawrence Erlbaum Associates, 2000).

29. See Henry Giroux, *Border Crossing*; Dennis Shirley et al., "Bringing the Community."

30. See Alan H. Bloomgarden and KerryAnn O'Meara, "Harmony or Cacophony? Faculty Role Integration and Community Engagement," *Michigan Journal of Community Service Learning* 13, no. 2 (2007): 5–18; KerryAnn O'Meara, "Encouraging Multiple Forms of Scholarship in Faculty Reward Systems: Does It Make a Difference?" *Research in Higher Education* 46, no. 5 (2005): 479–510; and Alice M. Buchanan, Shelia C. Baldwin, and Mary E. Rudisill, "Service Learning as Scholarship in Teacher Education," *Educational Researcher* 31, no. 5 (2002): 28–34.

31. Randy Stoecker, "Challenging Institutional Barriers to Community-Based Research," *Action Research* 6, no. 1 (2008): 51.

32. Dan W. Butin, "The Limits," 58.

33. Linda Darling-Hammond, "Educating."

34. Joel Westheimer, "Politics and Patriotism in Education," *Phi Delta Kappan* 87, no. 8 (2006): 607–20.

35. Irving Epstein, "Standardization and Its Discontents: The Standards Movement and Teacher Education in the Liberal Arts College Environment," in *Taking Teaching Seriously: How Liberal Arts Colleges Prepare Teachers to Meet Today's Educational Challenges*, ed. Christopher Bjork, D. Kay Johnston, and Heidi Ross (Boulder, CO: Paradigm Publishers, 2007), 31–50.

6

Asserting Community Engagement in Teacher Education

Community-engaged education is crucial for teacher preparation in twenty-first-century America. As the demographic and social realities of populations being served by schools change and more demands are made of them, university/college-based teacher education is increasingly being challenged to supply adequate and well-qualified teachers who are prepared to teach in these contexts.[1] At the same time, the so-called alternative programs see an opportunity to supply teachers to the nation's schools as national, state, and professional bodies continue to standardize teacher education and licensure through formulations of teacher quality standards and tests. Against this backdrop, schools, colleges, and departments of education (SCDEs) fight to balance the demands of providing a relevant professional teacher education and a higher education tradition that has historically privileged the "academic" at the expense of the "applied." It is against this background that I have urged in this book for a community-engaged approach to teacher education.

Several questions, however, still remain—among them: Can community engagement really become part of the core of a teacher education program in the twenty-first century? And how can such engagement be conceptualized to avoid the loopholes of past attempts to bring diverse communities into teacher education? In this chapter I examine three models that collectively provide insights into how community engagement may be conceptualized, and sometimes enacted, in teacher education at the program level. Although the three models examined here are not the only ones, they help make the point that the concept of community-engaged teacher education is not new, and that there have been moments, albeit fleeting, in the reform history when teacher education has sought to connect with diverse communities for teacher preparation. More importantly, their analyses can reveal key emphases of a community-engaged teacher education approach. In the following section, I discuss the three models, highlighting goals, challenges, and insights. I present key understandings that inform the community-engaged teacher education approach outlined in chapter 1 and examine the program, institutional, and external influences that may bear on this approach.

MODELS OF COMMUNITY ENGAGEMENT IN TEACHER EDUCATION: LINKING WITH FAMILIES AND COMMUNITY-BASED ORGANIZATIONS/AGENCIES

This model seeks to place preservice teachers in diverse communities as part of their education. Ideally, teacher education programs partner with community-based agencies or organizations to enable preservice teachers to learn about diverse communities as they assist in community activities. Perhaps one of the best known examples of broad-based, concerted efforts to link teacher education with diverse communities is the National Teacher Corps program. A brief discussion of the Teacher Corps program helps shed light on some of the features of this model. The Teacher Corps program was met with mixed responses when it was initiated in the mid-1960s. Some saw it as an appropriate extension into education of President Johnson's War on Poverty, others viewed it as a way to revitalize teacher education of the time, while still others cynically thought of it as one more government-sponsored reform initiative that was doomed to fail.[2] Those who saw it as a tool to fight poverty observed that "[it] was to do for the slums of America what the Peace Corps ideally did for the underdeveloped nation."[3] Writing about revitalizing teacher education, James Fraser noted:

> By recruiting young, well-educated idealists and placing them in teaching positions as interns, but also immersing them deeply in communities near their schools—something that few teacher education programs had done—and also engaging them in graduate courses in education programs to expand their teaching expertise, there was a hope that a new kind of teacher could be recruited and perhaps a new model developed that would in time transform even the education schools in the process.[4]

The Teacher Corps program was short-lived (1965–1981) and had limited effect. Many reasons have been advanced to explain the failure of this brief teacher education reform. One reason was that it received limited financial backing, as did other federal social programs of the time.[5] Other factors that fueled its demise included cynicism and frustration by interns, the inflexibility of existing systems to change, the undefined nature of the program, and the teacher glut of the late 1970s.[6]

This program, however, had several positive outcomes. One unexpected outcome of the Teacher Corps experiment was that it cast more attention on the teacher education curriculum, which had historically received limited federal attention. According to Penelope Earley, "Federal grants through this program, coupled with small federal investments in teaching and learning research agendas, led to the development and acceptance of a knowledge base for teacher education and greater legitimacy of the teacher education curriculum."[7] This knowledge base would include the knowledge for teaching in diverse contexts. This assertion is backed by Othanel Smith, who was commissioned by Teacher Corps to do a pedagogical study that resulted in the 1980 publication *A Design for a School of Pedagogy*, in which he emphasized community engagement as an important element of teacher education. Another remarkable aspect of the program was in its very nature: a deliberate attempt to attack an educational problem by attempting to forge a coalition among higher education, schools, and community. In this sense it was remarkable for its time. The emphasis on linking teacher education to the community was especially novel, but also the most challenging aspect of the program. Researcher Ronald Corwin observed:

> In concept, community work was one of the most innovative aspects of the Teacher Corps but, in practice, it was one of the most difficult, varied, and controversial phases of the program. Community activities that were observed were adaptations of traditional after-school, extracurricular activities with children, such as arts and crafts, clubs, and sports. Generally, insufficient time had been allotted to this phase of the program and, since it was not well incorporated into the daily routine, it was the first activity to be slighted. There was disagreement over the amount of encouragement that should be given to social action as opposed to social service and over the amount of encouragement that should be given to communitywide activities as opposed to activities directly related to classroom teaching. Also, teachers preferred for interns to assist in the classroom instead of to work in the community without supervision.[8]

Three related insights from the Teacher Corps experience can inform teacher education programs seeking to link with diverse communities for teacher preparation. First is the acknowledgment that interventions are needed to ameliorate inadequate education of diverse students. The Teacher Corps program stressed that such interventions would require conjoined efforts among teacher education programs, schools, and community. It acknowledged that diverse communities have typically been ignored in efforts to reform teacher education and schools, and emphasized that diverse communities are a resource for teacher education and teacher education programs are morally bound to help address community problems.

The second insight is that clarifying the nature and goal of community engagement is crucial. Teacher Corps had envisioned creating opportunities where interns would deeply participate in community activities, including home visits, projects requiring parent involvement, community health programs, cross-age student tutoring, recreation programs, revitalization of local PTAs, and parent or community education classes in child development.[9] However, this level of engagement was not realized and, as noted above, in most cases was replaced by activities offered within the service provider orientation.

The third insight is that community-based learning should be institutionalized if it is to meet desired goals. As noted above, in Teacher Corps curricular and conceptual integration of the community-based experiences in the teacher education curriculum did not work well throughout the program, partly due to a lack of buy-in from higher education faculty and the teachers involved. The lesson here is that integrating community-based field experiences is a challenging task which requires a particular mindset and certain programmatic and institutional supports. Funding is especially important to offset the cost involved in community engagement work, as it takes time and resources to design and provide adequate supervision for community-based experiences. These three insights are important for teacher education programs seeking to connect with diverse communities. They can be used to facilitate conversations about a program's beliefs about its role in society, as well as how community field experiences can be organized and sequenced to optimize learning for preservice teachers while relating with diverse communities in socially responsible and non-exploitative ways.

COLLABORATING WITH COMMUNITY SCHOOLS

In this model, community schools become centers for learning, teaching, learning to teach, and social action. In community schools, the boundaries between school and community are blurred, and prospective teachers complete their school/community-based learning within this context. As with teaching by regular teachers, their learning is tied to the broader goals of community development and social change. Teachers aim to teach to broader goals of education (including cultivating critical thinking, at-

tentiveness to diversity and equity, practicing culturally responsive pedagogy, and participation in a multicultural democratic society). Lee Benson
et al. describe the community school idea as one that is aligned with John
Dewey's notion of school as a social center, as a neighborhood site for
addressing social problems and enacting participatory democracy.[10] They
opine that Dewey's vision of the neighborhood school was "to function
as a publicly owned site, a publicly controlled and organized catalyst, to
bring people together and to develop coalitions of neighbors to solve the
multitude of problems suddenly emerging in advanced industrial societ-
ies."[11] Popular between 1960 and 1970, the idea of school as a social center
has been revived and kept alive through initiatives such as the full service
schools and the work of the Coalition for Community Schools.[12] Despite
this interest, the concept of school as social center has not become a significant part of the national discourse on education.[13] Nor has it impacted
teacher education in significant ways. Boyle-Baise and McIntyre examine
the history of community schools since the 1930s to present-day efforts by
The Coalition of Community Schools and lament that "while community
schools are well underway, efforts to prepare teachers to work in them
are almost non-existent."[14] Yet some teacher educators are convinced that
such schools present both an enduring solution to educational problems
in disenfranchised communities and a viable model for community engagement in higher education. Advocates of this model argue that when
higher education institutions participate in schools that are social centers,
they are in essence expressing their commitment to assist disenfranchised
communities to deal with educational failure, poverty, and other problems
facing the community. Lee Benson et al. speak to their realization of this
obligation in their involvement with a university-assisted community
school initiative at the University of Pennsylvania:

> We came to realize, more or less accidentally, that public schools, if strongly
> assisted by Penn, could effectively function as genuine community centers
> for the organization, education, and transformation of entire neighborhoods.
> They could do so by functioning as neighborhood sites for a West Phila-
> delphia Improvement Corps (WEPIC), consisting of school personnel and
> neighborhood residents who would receive strategic assistance from Penn
> students, faculty, and staff in their efforts to improve their schools and their
> quality of life.[15]

It is however important to underline that reciprocity is crucial to the
success of campus-community school partnerships; it requires that both
campus and community needs are addressed in an open and collaborative manner. Benson et al. report that engagement efforts have resulted
in changes on campus and in the community. For example, an interdisciplinary minor for undergraduates in Urban Education, offered through a

joint program of the School of Arts and Sciences and the Graduate School of Education, provide Penn students with opportunities for community service-learning and community-based research. As an example of meeting community needs, they offer the Sayre health clinic, which opened in 2006 as a result of efforts from both campus and community participants who worked to acquire funding to support this initiative located in a middle school.

Institutional commitment is another important ingredient for the success of community school partnerships. Development of centers and curricular integration are two important indicators of this commitment. The Penn community school initiative benefited from the assistantship provided by the Center for Community Partnerships, which was created in 1992 to provide direction and resources in designing community engagement courses. In addition to providing resources and logistical supports, the center facilitates curricular integration by enabling faculty across the disciplines to link their courses to the community school initiative. For example, in 2007 a total of 150 UPenn courses across disciplines were working with public schools and community organizations to solve strategic community problems; fifty-three of them were offered in the 2005–2006 academic year.[16]

Despite isolated instances of success like Penn's with university-assisted community schools, the literature indicates limited use of community schools for teacher education. The same applies to community schools that are not necessarily assisted by institutions of higher education.[17] It is possible, as Diana Pounder notes, that the numerous and documented challenges associated with interagency collaboration makes this option less desirable for teacher education.[18] In spite of the limited success of the community school model, important insights can be gleaned regarding community engagement with diverse communities.

The first insight is related to a basic tenet of community school partnerships: that higher education has an obligation to help schools, especially those serving low socioeconomic communities, to function as social centers. The second insight is that partnerships with community schools should be reciprocal and address the needs of the campus on one hand and school/community on the other. The third insight is that, due to the magnitude of involvement required to sustain community school partnerships, the responsibility must be extended beyond education departments. Such partnerships should involve the entire campus, and sufficient institutional supports should be made available toward this end. I concur with Lee Benson et al. when they posit that "previous experiments in community schools and community education throughout the country depended primarily on a single university unit, namely, the

School of Education. This was one major reason, we are convinced, for the failure, or limited success at best, of those experiments."[19] It is very difficult for a lone unit such as teacher education to successfully provide the level of partnership required in this model without support from other units in the institution. This is especially the case in small liberal arts colleges where departments of education are small and face unique challenges, some of which will be outlined in a later section. The three insights gleaned from this discussion of community school partnerships emphasize the depth of institutional commitment needed to support community-engaged teacher education efforts.

PARTNERSHIPS WITH COMMUNITY-ORIENTED PROFESSIONAL DEVELOPMENT SCHOOLS

The concept of community-oriented professional development schools (PDS), as envisioned by Boyle-Baise and McIntyre, stresses that PDS should include partnerships with communities. A brief explanation of the gaps in the typical conceptualization and practice of PDS helps put this emphasis on community orientation in perspective. PDS is understood both as a place and as a concept, and are characteristic of the "second wave" educational reforms that started in the mid-1980s.[20] As places, PDSs are located in public schools and collaborate with higher education, school districts, and professional agencies. As a concept, PDS emphasizes collaboration between schools and higher education for the simultaneous renewal of K–12 schools and teacher education. One important characteristic of this collaborative approach is that the two institutions partner around three main goals relating to teacher education: rethinking the preparation of preservice teachers, ensuring continued development of experienced teachers, and modeling exemplary practices based on inquiry that can foster K–12 student achievement.[21] While the PDS approach has popularized such concepts as collaboration, professionalism, and inquiry-based practices in teacher education, critics have pointed out that the lack of emphasis on partnerships with diverse communities ignores an important "player" in the renewal of teacher education and K–12 schools. For example, Peter Murrell has argued for the need to include urban communities in PDS partnerships:

> Although there is a general consensus that the renewal of teacher preparation will require the bridging of at least two types of professional communities— the community of schools, colleges, and departments of education (SCDEs) on the one hand, and school personnel on the other hand—the picture is still incomplete. . . . It is my contention that a third community of "players" is

essential to the renewal of teacher preparation, teacher quality, and school renewal. This is the community of adults who work with children in urban neighborhoods and centers of youth development. The most significant benefit of this partnership with urban communities is the opportunity for schools of education to draw on locally derived practical knowledge in order to develop vital, urban-focused, and community-committed teaching practices. . . . The success of urban school reform will depend, in part, on how the national agenda makes good on its enthusiasm for creating new "communities of learning," embracing diversity, and preparing teachers through community and collaborative partnership.[22]

Boyle-Baise and McIntyre, pursuing further some of the ideas presented by Murrell, suggest that expanding the concept of PDS can be done by broadening the understanding of teacher practice to include teacher understanding of the diverse communities served by the school; stressing partnerships among universities, schools, and communities; and encouraging an inquiry stance in preservice teachers by engaging them in cultural immersion, service projects, and community action research.[23] While the idea of community-oriented PDS remains in the theory stage, one can see its potential for shaping a community-engaged teacher education. It depicts teacher education as a collaborative effort among higher education, schools, and communities, and it views preservice teachers as active learners through inquiry-based learning activities in both school and community, with an emphasis on "attention to equity, diversity, family, and community needs."[24] This model stresses that community-based pedagogies can enhance the teaching profession.

This chapter began by posing two related questions: Can community engagement really become part of the core of a teacher education program in the twenty-first century? And how can such engagement be conceptualized to avoid the loopholes of past attempts to bring diverse communities into teacher education? I contend that for community engagement to become pervasive, teacher education programs will need to be informed by several understandings, some of which are gleaned from the analysis of the three models presented in the previous section and others from the discussion in preceding chapters.

A quick note here about my focus on understandings rather than models. While I appreciate the specificity provided by models, faithfulness to models can sometimes introduce constraints when parameters set by a model cannot apply to all contexts. Given that in the United States, university and college-based teacher education occurs in a broad range of contexts, a focus on understandings rather than models allows programs to interpret and implement them in ways that are possible within their given context. These understandings are summarized below:

- The impetus for community engagement should be a commitment to address the structural inequalities that result in educational disparities along race, class, language, and other forms of differences.
- Teacher education for diversity should involve a combination of university/college, school, *and* community-based activities. Collaboration across these sites is critical.
- Teachers need knowledge about diverse communities, in addition to subject matter expertise and pedagogical knowledge, to be effective. This knowledge should inform both curriculum and pedagogy.
- Community-based pedagogy in diverse communities enhances professional practice. Constructivist views of learning and teaching should guide this pedagogy.
- Community-based pedagogy is challenging to enact and requires certain programmatic and institutional supports.
- Teachers need to understand diverse students holistically as members of the school community, but also as belonging to families and communities with differing linguistic and cultural backgrounds. These differences should be viewed as resources rather than problems.
- Teachers should see themselves as organic members of the communities in which they teach. In addition to their work in the classrooms, they should participate in school-based, after-school, and community-based activities that connect them more organically to local realities from which their students come.
- Teachers should be agents of change. They should advocate for diverse students (as individuals and as a group) both in school and in the local communities.
- Teachers should aim to teach to broader goals of education, including cultivating critical thinking, attentiveness to diversity and equity, practicing culturally responsive pedagogy, and participation in a multicultural democratic society.
- Schools should seek to advance the intellectual development of their students, while also paying attention to the social, affective, health, cultural, moral, and political dimensions. A holistic approach to education is critical in diverse communities.
- Higher education and community partnerships should be reciprocal. Higher education can join with schools and communities in activities for the common good.

I believe that programs operating on the understandings outlined above are likely to increase their community engagement. It is, however, important to note that community-engaged programs are subject to program, institutional, and external influences; these are explored in the following section.

A CONSIDERATION OF PROGRAM, INSTITUTIONAL, AND EXTERNAL INFLUENCES

Program Influences

Jacqueline Irvine argues that organizational culture (that is, values, beliefs, and norms) influences program change. She elaborates that "values are represented in ideas and things perceived to be of importance, . . . beliefs are what one thinks is true, . . . norms are the way in which one perceives how things are done."[25] In particular, beliefs in four broad areas can influence a program's community engagement. These areas are: social responsibility of higher education; curriculum and pedagogy; responsibility to diverse communities; and the role of teachers and schools.

First is the program's belief about the role of higher education, specifically teacher education, in addressing the conditions that result in unequal schooling for K–12 students based on racial, class, linguistic, and other forms of socially constructed differences. In 1991, Liston and Zeichner offered a scathing criticism of teacher education's unresponsiveness to the inequality in our public school system:

> Despite all the attention to effective teaching, and the knowledge bases of teacher education, very little effort has been made within the teacher education community to try to ensure that all children will benefit from the excellence that we are promised, and that the proposed reforms are said to produce. The crisis of inequality in our public schools and the glaring inequities, injustices, and inhumanities in our society are barely even mentioned in the contemporary teacher education literature.[26]

Since the early 1990s, the language in teacher education has changed. It has become fashionable for teacher education programs to include in one form or another, teaching for social change/social justice as a goal.[27] More and more programs are now focusing on community engagement toward this goal. Community-engaged programs should not just state this goal, but should also adopt practices that are aligned with it. This alignment, as discussed in chapter 1, must be reflected in the vision, curriculum, and infrastructure. Programs lacking a shared vision for educating teachers for diversity through community engagement, the curricular emphasis on community-based pedagogy, and the necessary infrastructure to support this pedagogy are inadequately prepared for community engagement.

A program's beliefs about the best ways to structure curriculum and pedagogy with regard to educating for diversity can also influence its community engagement. Community-engaged programs acknowledge the importance of teaching content as well as the broader goals of education, including cultivating critical thinking, attending to diversity and equity, practicing culturally responsive pedagogy, and participating in a multicultural democratic society. Teacher educators in such programs are aware that campus- and school-based experiences alone are not sufficient to inculcate in preservice teachers the needed skills, dispositions, and knowledge for teaching with these emphases. They enhance this learning by including CFEs and providing opportunities for preservice teachers to reflect on their experience and make connections with academic theories. They seek to offer CFEs that are multifaceted and can enhance preservice teachers' understandings of skills for teaching diverse students, engaging with their families and communities, and developing "critical perspectives on the relationships between schooling and societal inequities, and a moral commitment to correcting those inequities through their daily classroom and school activities."[28] In chapter 2, I noted the need to provide more CFEs that go beyond service to equip preservice teachers with knowledge and skills for social critique and change. From the literature review it appears that few of these exist, in which case we need to be asking the important question: Who is served by CFEs in education? There is need to implement models of CFEs designed with social critique and social change as a starting point. When social critique and social change are the starting point, it is possible to avoid the charity or service-provider orientation ("often driven by a true sense of altruism, compassion, and joy, but unconsciously framed within noblesse oblige perceptions with ephemeral and shallow transformational value") which tends to inform many CFEs in education.[29]

In their emphasis on participation in meaning-making through practical experiences and reflection, teacher educators in engaged programs subscribe to the constructivist views of learning. As Villegas and Lucas noted, within constructivism, knowledge and the act of knowing are inseparable, and learning is an active process that has both intrapersonal and interpersonal components.[30] This form of learning is enduring. Preservice teachers exposed to community-based pedagogies are likely to use the same pedagogy in their classrooms to promote student understanding, respect for diversity, and active participation in communities and society. They are also likely to contribute significantly to broad-based school reform.[31] Community-engaged programs should espouse constructivism and emphasize CFEs as important educational experiences.

Beliefs about the importance of CFE pedagogy are closely related to beliefs about the responsibility of teacher education to diverse communities.

Community-engaged programs see diverse communities not as a source of problems but as valid sites for teacher preparation. Consistent with this perspective, they seek to form partnerships that acknowledge their responsibility, especially to the disenfranchised diverse communities that serve as sites for teacher education. Typical field experiences rarely interact with diverse communities in ways that ensure enduring benefit to these communities. Community-engaged programs should go beyond placing students in communities to developing relations that are collaborative and reciprocal. As noted in chapters 4 and 5, establishing healthy relationships with diverse communities requires deliberation and investment (in time and resources) on the side of teacher education. Lastly, beliefs about the role of teachers and schools in society can influence a program's engagement. Engaged programs seek to position teachers as organic leaders belonging to the communities in which they teach. Such teachers adopt the concept of difference as a resource and not as a problem. They participate in community-based activities that connect them to the lived realities of the families and communities from which their students come. And they are strong advocates for diverse students and their families. These teachers believe that schools should seek to advance the intellectual development of their students while also paying attention to the social, affective, health, cultural, moral, and political dimensions. They embrace a holistic approach to education.

In sum, teacher education programs that are likely to embrace community engagement have cultures that encourage an expansion of higher education's responsibility to diverse communities, that are committed to addressing disparities in K–12 schools, that recognize the power of community-based pedagogies in educating teachers for diversity, that seek reciprocity with diverse communities that serve as educational sites, and that embrace the transformative role of teachers and schools.

Institutional Influences

In addition to a program's culture, institutional factors can influence a teacher education program's capacity for community engagement. Foremost is the institution's relationship with neighboring communities. In small liberal arts colleges in particular, institutional support for community engagement has been slow compared to that in large higher education institutions. As was noted in chapter 1, this is despite the fact that many of these colleges were founded on social roots and their mission statements either directly or indirectly express a commitment to social change and/or social justice. Clearly, a mission that is supportive of social change, while essential, is insufficient to provide the institutional support needed for community engagement. Institutions that explicitly state their commitment and invest in structures that support community engagement are much more likely to positively influence community-engaged teacher education programs. Community-engaged teacher education programs also benefit when institutions address other indicators of community engagement such as supporting the institution-wide infusion of community engagement in the curriculum, utilizing campus resources to help communities address their needs, and incorporating community engagement in the faculty reward system.

Another institutional influence relates to the broader issue of teacher education status in the small liberal arts college.[32] In his well-regarded study of teacher education in different institutional contexts, Goodlad argued that even though teacher education in small liberal arts colleges possesses certain strengths when compared to its counterparts in other institutions, it does not share equal status with other academic departments.[33] He noted, "In the small liberal arts college, teacher education has a room at the inn but still sits at the bottom of the academic table. Preparing to teach is often lauded as a fine thing to do in such a college, but school teaching remains, nonetheless, the not-quite profession."[34] The low status implied here, compounded with what I refer to as 2Ps, can negatively influence community engagement in teacher education. The first P refers to prejudices against education faculty in small liberal arts colleges. According to Goodlad:

> It is interesting, however, that the propinquity of faculty members in a small college, often located in a small town, draws colleagues together. One tends to find the general-specific ambivalence of attitude reverses—that is, faculty members tend to see teacher education as a low-level intellectual enterprise but feel fortunate in having such able colleagues. It was fascinating to encounter this phenomenon in conversations with many administrators and arts and sciences faculty members on the campuses we visited. It gave me a new slant on the secondhand status of teacher education. The prevailing attitude suggested that although colleagues in the education department stray dangerously close to academic sin, they do so as if members of the Salvation Army.[35]

In addition to this "thinly veiled prejudice," teacher educators contend with a second P, which refers to the pressure caused by overwork, demands from accrediting agencies, and the low regard for education research amid the increasing "research-and-publication imperatives."[36] Community engagement, due to its low status in academia and its labor-intensive nature, can exacerbate these challenges.[37] Given such challenges, many education faculty are rightly concerned that community engagement may further jeopardize the status of teacher education or even their own survival in the small liberal arts college setting. All these institutional factors within the small liberal arts college context may actually deter education faculty from engaging in community-based work.

For community-engaged teacher education to succeed, institutional support for teacher education is needed at multiple levels. For example, an institution's commitment to community engagement can simultaneously bolster teacher education efforts by providing institutional supports, including resources to support community engagement and faculty reward systems that emphasize community engagement. Internally, institutions should strive to cultivate cultures that are respectful of teacher education in general. In institutions that are respectful of teacher education collaboration among faculty in education, the arts and sciences are fostered and all accept their role as teacher educators—after all, teacher candidates are expected to take courses in the arts and sciences as part of their teacher education. An institution-wide emphasis on community-based learning and research for both students and faculty can also go a long way to support community engagement in teacher education.

External Influences

"Teacher education in the US is under siege." Christine Sleeter made this alarming statement to draw attention to the fact that "[t]eacher education now finds itself under assault in the context of neoliberal pressures on education and society more broadly."[38] She argues that neoliberal pressures have resulted in conceptions of teacher education as "technical support for raising test scores"; a rendering of teacher professional knowledge as "questionable and even unnecessary"; and a de-emphasizing of college- and university-based teacher education.[39] Since the mid-1990s, a period which Cochran-Smith and Fries argue has been dominated by the "teacher education as a policy problem" perspective, the assumption has been that "one important way policy makers can meet the challenges of providing a high-quality teaching force is by manipulating those broad aspects of teacher preparation (e.g. teacher tests, subject matter requirements, entry routes) most likely to affect pupil achievement."[40] In this section, I examine how current and powerful political and economic contexts that, among other things, respond to neoliberal efforts toward accountability through high-stakes testing, narrowing the definition of teacher quality, and the undermining of college and university teacher education may hinder the growth of community engagement in teacher education.

An Increased Emphasis on Accountability through High-Stakes Testing

The emphasis in community-engaged teacher education to produce teachers who embrace the broader goals of education (including cultivating critical thinking, attentiveness to diversity and equity, practicing culturally responsive pedagogy, and participation in a multicultural democratic society), is not aligned with the current emphasis on accountability through high-stakes tests. With the influence of the No Child Left Behind (NCLB) Act, which was signed into law in 2002, schools are increasingly aligning themselves with state curriculum standards and high-stakes tests. Many see NCLB to be a culmination of efforts since A Nation at Risk (National Commission on Excellence in Education, 1983) to align education reform with the neoliberal agenda, which emphasizes global competition, standardization of curriculum and standardized testing, and deregulation of teacher education.[41] *In High-Stakes Testing: Coping with Collateral Damage*, Murray Thomas examines the "distressing mass of collateral damage" in learning and teaching resulting from the implementation of high-stakes testing, including teaching to the test, neglect of important fields of knowledge, information overload, and increased number of schools and students being dubbed as failures.[42] Also damaging is the "deskilling"[43] of teachers and the de-emphasis on educating for diversity that is implied by the emphasis on accountability through high-stakes testing.[44] Teachers are deskilled when their role is reduced to that of "technicians in the service of raising student test scores."[45] The diversity focus is jeopardized when educating for broader goals is seen to detract from the mandate of preparing teachers whose main focus is to serve the objectives of high-stakes tests and narrowly defined curriculum standards. The pressure exerted by the current emphasis on accountability through testing has also had a significant impact on teacher education. For example, Sleeter reviews literature that indicates that "it is increasingly difficult to find classroom field placements serving low-income students that model anything except scripted teaching, and some schools have threatened to stop working with schools of education that question the requirements of *No Child Left Behind* federal legislation."[46] Teacher education is increasingly likely to experience the pressure to prepare teachers who are in the service of state tests and narrowly defined curriculum. While teacher educators are supportive of testing as part of sound pedagogy, few believe that tests should detract from attentiveness to the broader goals of education; the two are not mutually exclusive. As community-engaged teacher education programs resist the pressure to narrow the role of teachers by equipping preservice teachers with a wide range of skills and knowledge needed to effectively teach diverse classrooms and teach to broader goals, they should expect a push back from preservice teachers, schools, state, and others who may not see this as necessary or urgent for K–12 teachers. Community-engaged teacher education programs, therefore, need to develop creative strategies for navigating the current educational reform terrain that is preoccupied with accountability through high-stakes tests, inattentive to diversity and equity, and narrowly defines the teacher's role.

The Changing Definitions of Teacher Quality and the
Politics of Teacher Certification

Certification or licensure regulations, which apply to teacher education programs across institutional contexts, are another external influence likely to impact community engagement in teacher education. David and Scott Imig, in their examination of the labyrinth of influences from federal and state level policies and numerous professional agencies that have historically vied to shape teacher preparation, note that NCLB has had a significant impact on teacher certification.[47] One impact relevant here is that many states are increasingly relying on two measures to define teacher quality for certification: "scores on standardized teacher tests, and degree attainment in a particular core or academic subject."[48] Concerns about this narrow definition of teacher knowledge among teacher educators are compounded by the growing influence of the "deregulation agenda," which promotes "greater access to teaching as the way to improve teacher quality, embracing both 'competitive' and 'alternative' certification as policy tools."[49] According to Zeichner,

> The deregulators have encouraged opening the gates to teaching, and support is offered for three different kinds of alternative certification options: (a) "missionary" programs, such as Teach for America, where the goal is to find idealistic and smart young people to spend a couple of years working in high-poverty schools before they move on to the corporate boardrooms and other leadership positions in society; (b) private for-profit alternatives offered by Sylvan Learning, Edison, and so on; and (c) school-based alternative routes in which districts prepare their own teachers.

He further points out that the deregulators seek

> to break what they see as the monopoly of colleges and teacher universities in initial teacher education programs by encouraging alternative certification programs and dismantling of state teacher certification. The argument is made that subject matter knowledge and teachers' verbal ability are the main determinants of teaching success, and it is asserted that much of what is offered in professional education methods and foundations courses can be learned on the job through apprenticeship.[50]

The growing influence of the deregulation agenda appears to many teacher educators to be further evidence of the narrowing of the definition of teacher quality. Many university/college teacher educators decry the distorted conceptions of professionalism and the blind faith in the market ideology that drive the deregulation agenda, as well as its inattentiveness to equity, diversity, social change, and other broader goals of education. Regarding equity concerns, for example, critics point out that many of the alternative route teachers are deployed in traditionally underserved schools with minimal training, while privileged schools continue to receive highly trained teachers from traditional teacher education programs. They also point to the contradiction in states relaxing standards for alternative programs while tightening requirements for college/university teacher education programs. As states continue to tighten requirements for college/university teacher education programs and alternative routes gain more ground, it is likely that programs will be tempted to concentrate only on what is perceived as valuable in certification requirements. In the game of survival, educating for diversity and emphasizing community engagement are likely to take a back seat.

The Questioning of College and University-Based Teacher Education

Although, as Zeichner notes, college- and university-based teacher education programs "continue to supply our nation's public schools with more teachers than any other source in most parts of the country," they are increasingly being questioned.[51] This questioning may threaten the leadership of college and university teacher education in teacher preparation, which obviously would restrict the growth of community-engaged teacher education. The questioning that Zeichner alludes to may be fueled by the current and powerful macro contexts that, among other things, respond to neoliberal efforts toward accountability through high-stakes testing, the narrowing of the definition of teacher quality, and the elimination of college and university teacher education. It may also in part be fueled by the perceived inability of college and university teacher education to respond adequately to the special challenge of providing teachers to schools that serve culturally diverse and low-income populations. Zeichner advises that teacher education can ignore this "questioning" at its own peril, and emphasizes the need "to make some changes in how we conduct our work in teacher education so that we make a greater contribution to preparing teachers who choose to teach in the schools and fields where they are most needed and who are successful and continue teaching in these schools."[52] If this advice is heeded, then teacher education will seek to educate for the diversity that is the reality in America's schools. I have proposed in this book that adopting a community-engaged approach can contribute toward this goal.

CONCLUSION

In these times when university/college-based teacher education is being severely tested, assaulted, and constricted through increasing diversity in K–12 and the impact of neoliberal policies on education, SCDEs need to be more vigilant than ever before to prepare effective teachers for all K–12 students. In this chapter I have argued that community-engaged teacher education is crucial for educating teachers who can effectively work in American's diverse K–12 classrooms. I examined three models (linking with families and community-based organizations or agencies, collaborating with community schools, and partnering with community-oriented PDS) to highlight several understandings that I believe can help community-engaged teacher education distinguish itself amid the numerous competing approaches in the field. Some of these understandings have also been highlighted previously. I have argued that programs that emphasize these understandings are likely to engage with diverse communities in ways that can be transformative for both diverse communities and teacher education programs. I have stressed that program, institutional, and external influences can impact the ability of teacher education to espouse these understandings. A program's culture can influence its community engagement, especially its beliefs about the social responsibility of higher education, effective curriculum and pedagogy for educating for diversity, teacher education responsibility to diverse communities, and the role of teachers and schools. Institutional influences that can impact engaged programs include the level of institutional community engagement, including centers to facilitate partnership work and faculty reward systems that acknowledge community-based work. Powerful sociopolitical contexts that, among other things, respond to neoliberal efforts to narrow the definition of teacher quality by reducing the role of the K–12 teacher to a technician in the service of high-stakes tests and promoting alternative routes to certification while undermining college- and university-based teacher education can also influence community engagement in teacher education.

CLOSING REMARKS

The purpose of this book was to articulate the possibility of linking teacher education with diverse communities for the purpose of educating teachers for diversity. How can teacher education take advantage of the current upsurge in the community engagement movement among higher education institutions (including the small liberal arts colleges) toward the goal of educating teachers for diversity? How can teacher education's vision and practices be modified to be more consistent with the goal of educating for cultural diversity through community engagement? How can the curriculum, especially the community-based field experiences (CFE) component in teacher education, be reconceptualized to both enhance program goals to educate for diversity and help meet the needs of diverse communities? What are some of the models that can productively infuse community-based learning experiences in the teacher education curriculum? How do faculty determine which of these models are in the service of diverse communities? What are the pedagogical implications of community engagement in teacher education? Is it necessary for teacher educators to forge healthy partnerships with diverse communities? How can teacher education programs help to deepen community engagement in their institutions? What are some of the program, institutional, and external influences that may hinder the community engagement in teacher education?

After reading the analyses of some of these questions in this book, I hope that readers can appreciate the urgency, potential, and challenges of the community-engaged approach to teacher education. The urgency lies in the need for teacher education to respond to realities in K–12 education and the disparities in educational outcomes for culturally diverse students. Because these disparities have consistently reflected racial, ethnic, class, language, and other differences, it is imperative that programs educate teachers who are socially responsible and culturally competent to respond to these educational inequities in their work as educators. While this focus has not historically been a priority for teacher education, I argue that the current emphasis on community engagement in higher education, and especially in small liberal arts institutions, can present invaluable opportunities for teacher education to strengthen the education of teachers for diversity. I stress a set of understandings that can guide programs toward deeper community-engagement. I also highlight some of the programmatic, institutional, and external challenges that can hinder the development of community-engaged teacher education.

NOTES

1. The literature indicates that few beginning teachers feel they are sufficiently prepared to teach in diverse classrooms. See, for example, Tamara Lucas and Jaime Grinberg, "Responding to the Linguistic Reality of Mainstream Classrooms: Preparing All Teachers to Teach English Language Learners," in *Handbook of Research on Teacher Education: Enduring Questions in Changing Contexts*, ed. Marilyn Cochran-Smith, Sharon Feiman-Nemser, D. John McIntyre, and Kelly Demers (New York: Routledge and Association of Teacher Educators, 2008), 606–36.

2. See Ronald G. Corwin, *Reform and Organizational Survival: The Teacher Corps as an Instrument of Educational Change* (New York: John Wiley & Sons, 1973); Penelope M. Earley, "Finding the Culprit: Federal Policy and Teacher Education," *Educational Policy* 14, no. 1 (January and March 2000): 25–39; James W. Fraser, *Preparing America's Teachers: A History* (New York: Teachers College Press, 2007).

3. Donald M. Sharpe, quoted in James W. Fraser, *Preparing America's Teachers*, 216.

4. James W. Fraser, *Preparing America's Teachers*, 216.

5. Penelope M. Earley, in "Finding the Culprit" notes that "Roughly 100 institutions received Teacher Corps Grants, and its highest appropriation level—in 1973—was $37.5 million, or less than one half of 1 percent of the appropriations for education and training in that fiscal year" (p. 29).

6. See James W. Fraser, *Preparing America's Teachers*; Ronald G. Corwin, *Reform and Organizational Survival*; Bethany L. Rogers, "Promises and Limitations of Youth Activism in the 1960s: The Case of the National Teacher Corps," *The Sixties: A Journal of History, Politics and Culture* 1, no. 2 (December 2008): 187–207.

7. Penelope M. Earley, "Finding the Culprit," 29.

8. Ronald G. Corwin, *Reform and Organizational Survival*, 152.

9. Ronald G. Corwin, *Reform and Organizational Survival*, 145.

10. Lee Benson, Ira Harkavy, and John Puckett, *Dewey's Dream: Universities and Democracies in an Age of Education Reform: Civil Society, Public Schools, and Democratic Citizenship* (Philadelphia, PA: Temple University Press, 2007), 125.

11. Benson, Harkavy, and Puckett, *Dewey's Dream*, 44.

12. See Joy G. Dryfoos, *Full Service Schools: A Revolution in Health and Social Services for Children, Youth, and Families* (San Francisco: Jossey-Bass Publishers, 1998); The Coalition of Community Schools defines community schools thus: "Using public schools as hubs, community schools bring together many partners to offer a range of supports and opportunities to children, youth, families and communities," http://www.communityschools.org/; according to Lee Benson, Ira Harkavy, and John Puckett in *Dewey's Dream*, "The Coalitions' increasing impact is effectively illustrated by the Full Service Community Schools Act, introduced in the U.S. House of Representatives in June 2004. . . . The act authorizes funding for full-service community schools that coordinate multiple federal, state, and local educational and social service programs in partnership with school districts, community-based organizations, and public-private partnerships" (p. 125).

13. For example, in a March 11, 2009 interview, Arne Duncan, the United States Secretary of Education, emphasized the concept of schools as a social center. He noted, "Where schools truly become the centers of the community, great things happen" http://www.charlierose.com/view/interview/10140#frame_top (accessed February 12, 2010).

14. Marilynne Boyle-Baise and D. John McIntyre, "What Kind of Experience? Preparing Teachers in PDS or Community Settings," in *Handbook of Research on Teacher Education*, 310.

15. Lee Benson, Ira Harkavy, and John Puckett, *Dewey's Dream*, 88.

16. Lee Benson, Ira Harkavy, and John Puckett, *Dewey's Dream*, 92.

17. See Joy G. Dryfoos, Jane Quinn, Carol Barkin, eds. *Community Schools in Action: Lessons from a Decade of Practice* (New York: Oxford University Press, 2005); Howell S. Baum, *Community Action for School Reform* (Albany, NY: State University of New York Press, 2003).

18. See Diana G. Pounder, ed., *Restructuring Schools for Collaboration: Promises and Pitfalls* (Albany: State University of New York Press, 1998).

19. Lee Benson, Ira Harkavy, and John Puckett, *Dewey's Dream*, 89.

20. Other names have been used instead of PDS to refer to these partnerships, including "partner schools," "clinical schools," and "professional practice schools." For a discussion on PDS as a concept and a place, see Ismat Abdal-Haqq, *Professional Development Schools: Weighing the Evidence* (Thousand Oaks, CA: Corwin Press, 1998).

21. Marilynne Boyle-Baise and D. John McIntyre, "What Kind of Experience"; Lucy Mule, "Preservice Teachers' Inquiry in a Professional Development School Context: Implications for the Practicum," in *Teaching and Teacher Education* 22, no. 2 (2006): 205–18.

22. Peter C. Murrell, *The Community Teacher: A New Framework for Effective Urban Teaching* (New York: Teachers College Press, 2001), 2.

23. Marilynne Boyle-Baise and D. John McIntyre, "What Kind of Experience," 324.

24. Marilynne Boyle-Baise and D. John McIntyre, "What Kind of Experience," 326.

25. Jacqueline Jordan Irvine, *Educating Teachers for Diversity: Seeing with a Cultural Eye* (New York: Teachers College Press, 2003), 18–25.

26. Daniel Patrick Liston and Kenneth M. Zeichner, *Teacher Education and the Social Conditions of Schooling* (New York: Routledge, 1991), xviii.

27. Kenneth M. Zeichner, *Teacher Education and the Struggle for Social Justice* (New York: Routledge, 2009), 93.

28. Kenneth M. Zeichner, *Teacher Education*, 33.

29. Anonymous reviewer. See also Marilynne Boyle-Baise, "Community Service-Learning for Multicultural Education: An Exploratory Study with Preservice Teachers," *Equity & Excellence of Education* 31 (1998): 52–60; Marilynne Boyle-Baise and Christine Sleeter, "Community-Based Service Learning for Multicultural Teacher Education," *Educational Foundations* 14 (2000): 33–50.

30. Ana María Villegas and Tamara Lucas, *Educating Culturally Responsive Teachers: A Coherent Approach* (Albany: State University of New York Press, 2002), 65–112.

31. See Carol Myers and Terry Pickeral, "Service-Learning: An Essential Process for Preparing Teachers as Transformational Leaders in the Reform of Public Education," in *Learning with the Community: Concepts and Models for Service Learning in Teacher Education*, ed. Joseph Erickson and Jeffrey Anderson (Sterling, VA: Stylus Publishing, LLC, 2005), 13–41.

32. For a discussion on education's status problem, see David F. Labaree, "An Uneasy Relationship: The History of Teacher Education in the University," in *Handbook of Research on Teacher Education*, 290–306.

33. See John. I. Goodlad, *Teachers for Our Nation's Schools* (San Francisco, CA: Jossey-Bass, 1990), 83. Goodlad argues that when compared to other higher education institutions (e.g., major research public universities, public major comprehensive universities, public regional universities and colleges, private major comprehensive universities and colleges, and private regional comprehensive universities and colleges), teacher education is better regarded in the small liberal arts college. He identifies factors in the small liberal arts colleges that appear favorable to the

education of teachers including a general intellectual environment, presence of a strong general education curriculum, a concern with moral and character development, less preoccupation with "research as king," a focus on excellent teaching, professor-student contact, and opportunities for prospective teachers to major in arts and sciences.

34. John I. Goodlad, *Teachers for Our Nation's Schools*, 83.

35. John I. Goodlad, *Teachers for Our Nation's Schools*, 80.

36. Education faculty, who are normally few compared to the number of students they serve in their courses, are often bogged down with developing relationships with public schools, and some, like those at Smith College, also support laboratory schools on their campuses. For special challenges facing education faculty in small liberal arts colleges, see John I. Goodlad, *Teachers for Our Nation's Schools*, 79–83; Charles Burgess, "Abiding by the 'Rule of Birds': Teaching Teachers in Small Liberal Arts Colleges," in *Places Where Teachers Are Taught*, ed. John I. Goodlad, Roger Soder, Kenneth A. Sorotnik (San Francisco, CA: Jossey-Bass, 1990), 87–135.

37. A large corpus of literature has explored the low prestige and lack of adequate institutional reward systems that are associated with community-engaged scholarship in higher education. See, for example, Alan H. Bloomgarden, "Civic Engagement and the 'Research College,'" in *Journal of Metropolitan Universities* 18, no. 1 (2007): 56–67; Alan H. Bloomgarden and KerryAnn O'Meara, "Harmony or Cacophony? Faculty Role Integration and Community Engagement," *Michigan Journal of Community Service Learning* 13, no. 2 (2007): 5–18; KerryAnn O'Meara, "Encouraging Multiple Forms of Scholarship in Faculty Reward Systems: Does It Make a Difference?" *Research in Higher Education* 46, no. 5 (2005): 479–510; "Reframing Incentives and Rewards for Community Service-Learning and Academic Outreach," in *Journal of Higher Education Outreach and Engagement* 8, no. 2 (2003): 201–20; and KerryAnn O'Meara and Eugene R. Rice, eds., *Faculty Priorities Reconsidered: Rewarding Multiple Forms of Scholarship* (San Francisco, CA: Jossey-Bass, 2005).

38. Christine Sleeter, "Equity, Democracy, and Neoliberal Assaults on Teacher Education," *Teaching and Teacher Education* 24 (2008): 1947–57. Christine Sleeter uses Harvey (2005) to define neoliberalism as "a theory of political economic practices that proposes that human well-being can best be advanced by liberating individual entrepreneurial freedoms and skills within an institutional framework characterized by strong private property rights, free markets, and free trade" (p. 1947).

39. Christine Sleeter, "Equity, Democracy, and Neoliberal Assaults" (p. 1951–54).

40. Marilyn Cochran-Smith and Kim Fries, "Research on Teacher Education: Changing Times, Changing Paradigms," in *Handbook of Research on Teacher Education: Enduring Questions in Changing Contexts*, ed. Marilyn Cochran-Smith, Sharon Feiman-Nemser, D. John McIntyre, and Kelly Demers (New York: Routledge and Association of Teacher Educators, 2008), 1082.

41. See David Hursh, "Assessing No Child Left Behind and the Rise of Neoliberal Education Policies," *American Educational Research Journal* 44, no. 3 (September 2007): 493–518; Linda Darling-Hammond, "Race, Inequality and Educational Ac-

countability: The Irony of 'No Child Left Behind," *Race, Ethnicity and Education* 10, no. 3 (September 2007): 245–60; Michael W. Apple, "Markets, Standards, Teaching, and Teacher Education," *Journal of Teacher Education* 52, no. 3 (May/June 2001): 182–96; Christine Sleeter, "Equity, Democracy, and Neoliberal Assaults."

42. See R. Murray Thomas, *High-Stakes Testing: Coping with Collateral Damage* (Mahwah, NJ: Lawrence Erlbaum Associates, 2005).

43. Stella C. Batagiannis, "The Quest for Instantaneous Perfection and the Demand for 'Push-Button' Administration," *The Educational Forum* 73, no. 1 (January 2009): 33–43.

44. Critics have charged that although NCLB, by emphasizing disaggregate test scores, has revealed the glaring disparities in achievement among various categories based on race, language, class, and disability, it has neglected to deliver on equity goals. For instance, NCLB pays little attention to addressing the structural inequalities that result in these disparities. Furthermore, high-stakes tests can play the gatekeeping role that disadvantages diverse populations. Indeed, some critics see NCLB as a threat to educational equity gains of the civil rights era, noting that past policies that have affirmed diversity such as the bilingual education and multicultural education have come under assault under this law.

45. Christine Sleeter, "Equity, Democracy, and Neoliberal Assaults on Teacher Education,"1952.

46. Christine Sleeter, "Equity, Democracy, and Neoliberal Assaults on Teacher Education," 1952.

47. See David G. Imig and Scott R. Imig, "From Traditional Certification to Competitive Certification," in *Handbook of Research on Teacher Education: Enduring Questions in Changing Contexts*, ed. Marilyn Cochran-Smith, Sharon Feiman-Nemser, D. John McIntyre, and Kelly Demers (New York: Routledge and Association of Teacher Educators, 2008), 886–907.

48. David G. Imig and Scott R. Imig, "From Traditional Certification to Competitive Certification," 899.

49. David G. Imig and Scott R. Imig, "From Traditional Certification to Competitive Certification," 899.

50. Kenneth M. Zeichner, "Teacher Education," 13–14.

51. Kenneth M. Zeichner, "Teacher Education," 149.

52. Kenneth M. Zeichner, "Teacher Education," 149.

Bibliography

Abdal-Haqq, Ismat. *Professional Development Schools: Weighing the Evidence.* Thousand Oaks, CA: Corwin Press, 1998.

Adams, Maurianne, Lee A. Bell, and Pat Griffin, eds. *Teaching for Diversity and Social Justice: A Sourcebook.* New York: Routledge, 1997.

Adger, Carolyn Temple. "School-Community-Based Organization Partnership for Language Minority Students' School Success." *Journal of Education for Students Placed at Risk* 6, nos. 1 and 2 (2001): 7–25.

Adler-Kassner, Linda, Robert Crooks, and Ann Watters, eds. *Writing the Community: Concepts and Models for Service Learning in Composition.* Sterling, VA: Stylus, 2006.

Albert, Gail. "Intensive Service-Learning Experiences." Pp. 182–207 in *Service-Learning in Higher Education: Concepts and Practices*, edited by Barbara Jacoby and Associates. San Francisco: Jossey-Bass, 1996.

Anderson, James D. *The Education of Blacks in the South 1860–1935.* Chapel Hill: University of North Carolina Press, 1988.

Anderson, Jeffrey B., and Joseph A. Erickson. "Service-Learning in Preservice Teacher Education." *Academic Exchange* (Summer 2003): 111–15.

Anderson, Jeffrey B., Kevin J. Swick, and Joost Yff, eds. *Service-Learning in Teacher Education: Enhancing the Growth of New Teachers, Their Students, and Communities.* Washington, DC: American Association of Colleges for Teacher Education (AACTE), 2001.

Asante, Molefi K. *The Afrocentric Idea.* Philadelphia: Temple University Press, 1987.

Association of Teacher Education (ATE). "Standards for Teacher Educators." http://www.atel.org/pubs/uploads/tchredstds 0308.pdf (accessed September 15, 2008).

Au, Kathryn H., and Karen M. Blake. "Cultural Identity and Learning to Teach in a Diverse Community: Findings from a Collective Case Study." *Journal of Teacher Education* 54, no. 3 (May–June 2003): 192–205.

Baldwin, Shelia C., Alice M. Buchanan, and Mary E. Rudisill. "What Teacher Candidates Learned about Diversity, Social Justice, and Themselves from Service-Learning Experiences." *Journal of Teacher Education* 58, no. 4 (2007): 315–27.

Ball, Arnetha F. "Empowering Pedagogies That Enhance Multicultural Students." *Teachers College Record* 102, no. 6 (2000): 1006–34.

Ball, Arnetha F., and Ted Lardner. *African American Literacies Unleashed: Vernacular English and the Composition Class*. Carbondale, IL: Southern Illinois University Press, 2005.

Balliet, Barbara, and Kerisaa Heffernan, eds. *The Practice of Change: Concepts and Models for Service-Learning in Women's Studies*. Washington, DC: American Association for Higher Education (AAHE), 2000.

Banks, James, Marilyn Cochran-Smith, Luis Moll, Anna Richert, Kenneth Zeichner, Pamela Lepage, Linda Darling-Hammond, Helen Duffy, and Morva McDonald. "Teaching Diverse Learners." Pp. 232–74 in *Preparing Teachers for a Changing World*, edited by Linda Darling-Hammond and John Bransford. San Francisco: Jossey-Bass, 2005.

Barber, Benjamin R., and Richard Battistoni. "A Season of Service: Introducing Service Learning into the Liberal Arts Curriculum." *PS: Political Science and Politics* 26, no. 2 (June 1993): 235–40.

Battisoni, Richard. "Service Learning and Civic Education." Pp. 29–44 in *Education for Civic Engagement in Democracy: Service-Learning and Other Promising Practices*, edited by Sheila Mann and John Patrick. Bloomington, IN: Eric Clearinghouse for Social Studies/Social Science Education, 2000.

Baum, Howell S. *Community Action for School Reform*. Albany, NY: State University of New York Press, 2003.

Bell, Lee Anne. "Theoretical Foundations for Social Justice Education." Pp. 3–15 in *Teaching for Diversity and Social Justice: A Sourcebook*, edited by Maurianne Adams, Lee Anne Bell, and Pat Griffin. New York: Routledge, 1997.

Benson, Lee, Ira Harkavy, and John Puckett. *Dewey's Dream: Universities and Democracies in an Age of Education Reform: Civil Society, Public Schools, and Democratic Citizenship*. Philadelphia: Temple University Press, 2007.

Berrien, Jacqueline. "A Civil Liberties Imperative: Promoting Quality Education for All African-American Children." *Teachers College Record* 94, no. 4 (1993): 790–99.

Bjork, Christopher, D. Kay Johnston, and Heidi Ross. *Taking Teaching Seriously: How Liberal Arts Colleges Prepare Teachers to Meet Today's Educational Challenges*. Boulder, CO: Paradigm Publishers, 2007.

Bloomgarden, Alan H. "Civic Engagement and the 'Research College.'" *Journal of Metropolitan Universities* 18, no. 1 (2007): 56–67.

Bloomgarden, Alan H., and KerryAnn O'Meara. "Harmony or Cacophony? Faculty Role Integration and Community Engagement." *Michigan Journal of Community Service Learning* 13, no. 2 (2007): 5–18.

Bondy, Elizabeth, and Steven Davis. "The Caring of Strangers: Insights from a Field Experience in a Culturally Unfamiliar Community." *Action in Teacher Education* 22, no. 2 (summer 2000): 54–66.

Boyer, Ernest L. "Creating the New American College." *The Chronicle of Higher Education* 40, no. 27 (1994): A48.

——. "The Scholarship of Engagement." *Journal of Public Service and Outreach* 1, no. 1 (1996): 11–20.

——. "The Scholarship of Engagement." *Bulletin of the American Academy of Arts and Sciences* 49, no. 7 (1996): 18–33.

Boykin, A. Wade, Robert J. Jagers, Constance M. Ellison, and Aretha Albury. "Communalism: Conceptualization and Measurement of an Afrocultural Social Orientation." *Journal of Black Studies* 27, no. 3 (1997): 409–18.

Boyle-Baise, Marilynne. *Multicultural Service-Learning: Educating Teachers in Diverse Communities*. New York: Teachers College Press, 2002.

——. "Preparing Community-Oriented Teachers: Reflections from a Multicultural Service-Learning Project." *Journal of Teacher Education* 56, no. 5 (2005): 446–58.

Boyle-Baise, Marilynne, and Patricia Efiom. "The Construction of Meaning: Learning from Service-Learning." Pp. 209–26 in *Integrating Service-Learning and Multicultural Education in Colleges and Universities*, edited by Carolyn R. O'Grady. Mahwah, NJ: Lawrence Erlbaum Associates, 2000.

Boyle-Baise, Marilynne, Bart Epler, and William McCoy. "Shared Control: Community Voices in Multicultural Service Learning." *The Educational Forum* 65, no. 4 (2001): 344–53.

Boyle-Baise, Marilynne, and D. John McIntyre. "What Kind of Experience? Preparing Teachers in PDS or Community Settings." Pp. 307–30 in *Handbook of Research on Teacher Education: Enduring Questions in Changing Contexts*, edited by Marilyn Cochran-Smith, Sharon Feiman-Nemser, D. John McIntyre, and Kelly Demers. New York: Routledge and Association of Teacher Educators, 2008.

Bringle, Robert G., Richard Games, and Edward A. Malloy. *Colleges and Universities as Citizens*. Boston: Allyn and Bacon, 1999.

Bringle, Robert G., and Julie Hatcher. "Campus-Community Partnerships: The Terms of Engagement." *Journal of Social Issues* 58, no. 3 (2002): 503–16.

——. "Institutionalization of Service Learning in Higher Education." *Journal of Higher Education* 17, no. 3 (2000): 273–90.

Bringle, Robert G., Julie Hatcher, and Richard Games. "Engaging and Supporting Faculty in Service-Learning." *Journal of Public Service and Outreach* 2, no. 1 (1997): 43–51.

Brown, Danika M. "Pulling It Together: A Method for Developing Service-Learning and Community Partnerships Based in Critical Pedagogy." 2001. www.nationalserviceresources.org/filemanager/download/453/brown.pdf (accessed January 15, 2008).

Brukardt, Mary Jane, Barbara Holland, Stephen Percy, and Nancy Zimpher. "The Path Ahead: What's Next for University Engagement?" Pp. 242–61 in *Creating a New Kind of University: Institutionalizing Community-University Engagement*, edited by Stephen Percy, Nancy Zimpher, and Mary Jane Brukardt. Bolton, MA: Anker Publishing Company, Inc., 2006.

Bruner, Jerome. "Life as Narrative." Pp. 28–37 in *The Need for Story: Cultural Diversity in Classroom and Community*, edited by Anne Haas Dyson and Celia Genishi. Urbana, IL: National Council of Teachers of English, 1994.

———. "The Narrative Construction of Reality." *Critical Inquiry* 18, no. 1 (1991): 1–21.

Buchanan, Alice M., Shelia C. Baldwin, and Mary E. Rudisill. "Service Learning as Scholarship in Teacher Education." *Educational Researcher* 31, no. 5 (2002): 28–34.

Buck, Patricia, and Paul Skilton Sylvester. "Preservice Teachers Enter Urban Communities: Coupling Funds of Knowledge Research and Critical Pedagogy in Teacher Education." Pp. 213–32 in *Funds of Knowledge: Theorizing Practices in Households, Communities, and Classrooms*, edited by Norma Gonzáles, Luis C. Moll, and Cathy Amanti. Mahwah, NJ: Lawrence Erlbaum Associates, Publishers, 2005.

Burant, Terry J., and Dan Kirby. "Beyond Classroom-Based Early Field Experiences: Understanding an Educative Practicum in an Urban School and Community." *Teaching and Teacher Education* 18 (2002): 561–75.

Burgess, Charles. "Abiding by the 'Rule of Birds': Teaching Teachers in Small Liberal Arts Colleges." Pp. 87–135 in *Places Where Teachers Are Taught*, edited by John I. Goodlad, Roger Soder, and Kenneth A. Sorotnik. San Francisco: Jossey-Bass, 1990.

Busch, Amy E., and Arnetha F. Ball. "Lifting Voices in the City." *Educational Leadership* 62, no. 2 (2002): 64–67.

Butin, Dan W. "The Limits of Service-Learning in Higher Education." *The Review of Higher Education* 29, no. 4 (2006): 473–98.

———. "Of What Use Is It? Multiple Conceptualizations of Service Learning Within Education." *Teachers College Record* 105, no. 9 (2003): 1674–92.

———. *Service-Learning in Higher Education: Critical Issues and Direction.* New York: Palgrave Macmillan, 2005.

———. "Disciplining Service Learning: Institutionalization and the Case for Community Studies. *International Journal of Teaching and Learning in Higher Education* 18, no. 1 (2006): 57–64.

Byrne, Jamie M. "University Intervention into Community Issues as Dialogic Public Relations: A Case Study." *Journal of Metropolitan Universities* 18, no. 1 (2007): 30–42.

Callahan, Jane, and Lynn Ryan. "Program Models: Providence College." Pp. 221–25 in *Learning with the Community: Concepts and Models for Service-Learning in Teacher Education*, edited by Joseph Erickson and Jeffery B. Anderson. Sterling, VA: Stylus Publishing, LLC. 2005.

Calleson, Diane C., Catherine Jordan, and Sarena D. Seifer. "Community-Engaged Scholarship: Is Faculty Work in Communities a True Academic Enterprise?" *Academic Medicine* 80, no. 4 (2005): 317–21.

Carlisle, Lenore Reilly, Bailey W. Jackson, and Allison George. "Principles of Social Justice Education: The Social Justice Education in Schools Project." *Equity & Excellence in Education* 39, no. 1 (2006): 55–64.

Carter, Kathy, and Walter Doyle. "Narrative and Learning to Teach: Implications for Teacher-Education Curriculum." *Journal of Curriculum Studies* 35, no. 2 (2003): 129–37.

Cass, Julia. "The Moses Factor." http://www.typp.org/media/docs/6245_ TheMosesFactor(motherjones).pdf (accessed January 31, 2007).

Cisneros, Henry G. "The University and the Urban Challenge." *Cityscape: A Journal of Policy Development and Research* (December 1996). http://www.huduser .org/Periodicals/CITYSCPE/SPISSUE/ch1.pdf (accessed June 20, 2009).

Cochran-Smith, Marilyn. "Learning to Teach Against the (New) Grain." *Journal of Teacher Education* 52, no. 1 (2001): 3–4.

———. "Learning to Teach for Social Justice." Pp. 114–44 in *The Education of Teachers: Ninety-Eight Yearbook of the National Society for the Study of Education*, edited by Gary A. Griffin. Chicago: The National Society for the Study of Education, 1999.

———. "The Multiple Meanings of Multicultural Teacher Education: A Conceptual Framework." *Teacher Education Quarterly* 30, no. 2 (2003): 7–26.

———. *Walking the Road: Race, Diversity, and Social Justice in Teacher Education.* New York: Teachers College Press, 2004.

Cochran-Smith, Marilyn, Sharon Feiman-Nemser, D. John McIntyre, and Kelly E. Demers, eds. *Handbook of Research on Teacher Education: Enduring Questions in Changing Contexts.* New York: Routledge and Association of Teacher Educators, 2008.

Cochran-Smith, Marilyn, and Kim Fries. "The AERA Panel on Research and Teacher Education: Context and Goals." Pp. 1–68 in *Studying Teacher Education: The Report of the AERA Panel on Research and Teacher Education*, edited by Marilyn Cochran-Smith and Kenneth M. Zeichner. Mahwah, NJ: Lawrence Erlbaum Associates, Inc., 2005.

Cochran-Smith, Marilyn, and Kenneth M. Zeichner, eds. *Studying Teacher Education: The Report of the AERA Panel on Research and Teacher Education.* Mahwah, NJ: Lawrence Erlbaum Associates, 2005.

Comer, James P. "The Potential Effects of Community Organizations on the Future of Our Youth." *Teachers College Record* 94, no. 3 (1993): 658–61.

———. *Waiting for a Miracle: Why Schools Can't Solve Our Problems—and How We Can.* New York: Plume, 1998.

Cooper, Patricia M. "Effective White Teachers of Black Children: Teaching Within a Community." *Journal of Teacher Education* 54, no. 95 (2003): 413–27.

Cowhey, Mary. *Black Ants and Buddhists: Thinking and Teaching Differently in Primary Grades.* Portland, ME: Stenhouse Publishers, 2006.

Cuban, Sondra, and Jeffrey B. Anderson. "Where's the Justice in Service-Learning? Institutionalizing Service-Learning from a Social Justice Perspective at a Jesuit University." *Equity & Excellence in Education* 40, no. 2 (2007): 144–55.

Cummings, C. Kim. "John Dewey and the Rebuilding of Urban Community: Engaging Undergraduates as Neighborhood Organizers." *Michigan Journal of Community Service Learning* 7, no. 1 (2001): 97–109.

Cushman, Ellen. "Sustainable Service Learning Programs." *College Composition and Communication* 54, no. 1 (2002): 40–65.

Daigre, Eric. "Toward a Critical Service-Learning Pedagogy: A Freirean Approach to Civic Literacy." *Academic Exchange Quarterly* 4, no. 4 (2000). http://www .thefreelibrary.com/Academic+Exchange+Quarterly/2000/December/22 -p568 (accessed June 15, 2009).

Darling-Hammond, Linda. "Constructing 21st Century Teacher Education." *Journal of Teacher Education* 57, no. 3 (May/June 2006): 300–14.

———. "Educating a Profession for Equitable Practice." Pp. 210–12 in *Learning to Teach for Social Justice*, edited by Linda Darling-Hammond, J. Jennifer French, and Silvia Paloma Garcia-Lopez. New York: Teachers College, Columbia University, 2002.

———. *Professional Development Schools: Schools for Developing a Profession.* New York: Teachers College Press, 1994.

———. *Powerful Teacher Education.* San Francisco: Jossey-Bass, 2005

———. "Teacher Quality and Student Achievement: A Review of State Policy Evidence." *Educational Policy Analysis Archives* 8, no. 1 (2000). http://epaa.asu .edu/epaa/v8n1/ (accessed May 2007).

Darling-Hammond, Linda, and John Bransford. *Preparing Teachers for a Changing World: What Teachers Should Learn and Be Able to Do.* San Francisco: Jossey-Bass, 2005.

Darling-Hammond, Linda, Ruth Chung, and Fred Frelow. "Variation in Teacher Preparation: How Well Do Different Pathways Prepare Teachers to Teach?" *Journal of Teacher Education* 53, no. 4 (2002): 286–302.

Deans, Tom. "Writing Across the Curriculum and Community Service Learning: Correspondences, Cautions and Futures." Pp. 29–37 in *Writing the Community: Concept Models for Service-Learning in Composition*, edited by Linda Adler-Kassner, Robert Crooks and Ann Watters. AAHE Series on Service-Learning in the Disciplines. Washington, DC: AAHE/Co-Published by NCTE, 1997.

DeBlasis, Amy Lee. "From Revolution to Evolution: Making the Transition from Community Service Learning to Community-Based Research." *International Journal of Teaching and Learning in Higher Education* 18, no. 1 (2006): 36–42.

Deshano da Silva, Carol, James Huguley, Zenub Kakli, and Radhika Rao, eds. *The Opportunity Gap: Achievement and Inequality in Education.* Cambridge, MA: Harvard Education Press, 2007.

Dodd, Ann Wescott, and Jean L. Konzal. *How Communities Build Stronger Schools: Stories, Strategies, and Promising Practices for Educating Every Child.* New York: Palgrave Macmillan, 2002.

Dodd, Elizabeth L., and Dana H. Lilly. "Learning Within Communities: An Investigation of Community Service-Learning in Teacher Education." *Action in Teacher Education* 22, no. 3 (Fall 2000): 77–85.

Donahue, David, Jane Boyer, and Dana Rosenberg. "Learning with and Learning From: Reciprocity in Service Learning in Teacher Education." *Equity & Excellence in Education* 36, no. 1 (2003): 15–17.

Doyle, Walter. "Heard Any Really Good Stories Lately? A Critique of the Critics of Narrative in Educational Research." *Teaching and Teacher Education* 13, no. 1 (1997): 93–99.

Droge, David, and Bren Ortega, eds. *Voices of Strong Democracy: Concepts and Models for Service Learning in Communication Studies.* Washington, DC: American Association for Higher Education (AAHE), 1999.

Dryfoos, Joy G., Jane Quinn, and Carol Barkin, eds. *Community Schools in Action: Lessons from a Decade of Practice.* New York: Oxford University Press, 2005.

Ducharme, Edward R. "A Response to Chapter 3, 'Right-Sizing Teacher Education: The Policy Imperative' by Nancy L. Zimpher." Pp. 63–72 in *Teachers for the New Millennium: Aligning Teacher Development, National Goals, and High Standards for All Students*, edited by Leonard Kaplan and Roy A. Edelfelt. Thousand Oaks, CA: Corwin Press, 1996.

Ducharme, Mary, and Edward Ducharme. "A Study of Teacher Educators: Research from the USA." *Journal of Education for Teaching* 22, no. 1 (1996): 57–70.

Dunlap, Michelle R. "Voices of Students in Multicultural Service-Learning Settings." *Michigan Journal of Community Service Learning* (Fall 1998): 58–67.

Earley, Penelope M. "Finding the Culprit: Federal Policy and Teacher Education." *Educational Policy* 14, no. 1 (2000): 25–39.

Ehrlich, Thomas, ed. *Civic Responsibility and Higher Education*. Phoenix, AZ: Oryx Press, 2000.

Eisner, Elliot W. *The Kind of Schools We Need: Personal Essays*. Portsmouth, NH: Heinemann, 1998.

Enos, Sandra, and Keith Morton. "Developing a Theory and Practice of Campus-Community Partnerships." Pp. 20–41 in *Building Partnerships for Service Learning*, edited by Barbara Jacoby. San Francisco: Jossey-Bass, 2003.

Epstein, Irving. "Standardization and Its Discontents: The Standards Movement and Teacher Education in the Liberal Arts College Environment." Pp. 31–50 in *Taking Teaching Seriously: How Liberal Arts Colleges Prepare Teachers to Meet Today's Educational Challenges*, edited by Christopher Bjork, D. Kay Johnston, and Heidi Ross. Boulder, CO: Paradigm Publishers, 2007.

Epstein, Joyce. *School, Family, and Community Partnerships: Preparing Educators and Improving Schools*. Boulder, CO: Westview Press, 2001.

Epstein, Joyce L., and Mavis Sanders. "Prospects for Change: Preparing Educators for School, Family, and Community Partnerships." *Peabody Journal of Education* 81, no. 2 (2006): 81–120.

Erickson, Joseph, and Jeffrey Anderson, eds. *Learning with the Community: Concepts and Models for Service Learning in Teacher Education*. Sterling, VA: Stylus Publishing, LLC, 2005.

Fenstermacher, Gary D. "The Knower and the Known: The Nature of Knowledge in Research on Teaching." *Review of Research in Education* 20, no. 1 (1994): 3–56.

Ference, Ruth A., and Steven Bell. "A Cross-Cultural Immersion in the U.S.: Changing Preservice Teacher Attitudes toward Latino ESOL Students." *Equity & Excellence in Education* 37, no. 4 (2004): 343–50.

Ferguson, Ronald. *Toward Excellence with Equity: An Emerging Vision for Closing the Achievement Gap*. Cambridge, MA: Harvard Education Press, 2007.

Fraser, James W. *Preparing America's Teachers: A History*. New York: Teachers College Press, 2007.

———. "Preparing Teachers for Democratic Schools: The Holmes and Carnegie Reports Five Years Later—A Critical Reflection." *Teachers College Record* 94, no. 1 (Fall 1992): 7–40.

Freire, Paulo. *Pedagogy of the Oppressed*. New York: Continuum, 1970.

———. *Teachers as Cultural Workers: Letters to Those Who Dare Teach*. Boulder: Westview Press, 1998.

Freire, Paulo, and Myles Horton. *We Make the Road by Walking: Conversations on Education and Social Change.* Philadelphia: Temple University Press, 1990.

Futrell, Mary. "Changing Paradigm: Preparing Teacher Educators and Teachers for the Twenty-First Century." Pp. 534–39 in *Handbook of Research on Teacher Education: Enduring Questions in Changing Contexts,* edited by Marilyn Cochran-Smith, Sharon Feiman-Nemser, D. John McIntyre, and Kelly E. Demers. New York: Routledge and Association of Teacher Educators, 2008.

Futrell, Mary H., Joel Gomez, and Dana Bedden. Teaching the Children of a New America: The Challenge of Diversity. *Phi Delta Kappan* (January 2003): 381–85.

Gallagher, Karen S., and Jerry D. Bailey, eds. *The Politics of Teacher Education Reform: The National Commission on Teaching and America's Future.* Thousand Oaks, CA: Corwin Press, 2000.

Gallego, Margaret. "Is Experience the Best Teacher? The Potential of Coupling Classroom and Community-Based Field Experiences." *Journal of Teacher Education* 52, no. 4 (2001): 312–25.

Gay, Geneva. *Culturally Responsive Teaching: Theory, Research and Practice.* New York: Teachers College Press, 2000.

———. "Preparing for Culturally Responsive Teaching." *Journal of Teacher Education* 53, no. 2 (2002): 106–17.

———. *A Synthesis of Scholarship in Multicultural Education.* Naperville, IL: North Central Regional Educational Laboratory, 2005.

Giroux, Henry. *Border Crossings: Cultural Workers and the Politics of Education.* New York: Routledge, 2005.

———. *Teachers as Intellectuals: Toward a Critical Pedagogy of Learning.* Westport, CT: Bergin & Garvey Publishers, Inc., 1988.

Goldblatt, Eli. "Alinsky's Reveille: A Community-Organizing Model for Neighborhood-Based Literacy Projects." *College English* 67, no. 3 (January 2005): 274–95.

Goodlad, John I. *Teachers for Our Nation's Schools.* San Francisco: Jossey-Bass, 1990.

Goodlad, John I., Roger Soder, and Kenneth A. Sorotnik, eds. *Places Where Teachers Are Taught.* San Francisco: Jossey-Bass, 1990.

González, Norma, Luis C. Moll, and Cathy Amanti, eds. *Funds of Knowledge: Theorizing Practices in Households, Communities, and Classrooms.* Mahwah, NJ: L. Erlbaum Associates, 2005.

Gordon, June. A. *The Color of Teaching.* New York: Routledge and Falmer, 2000.

———. "The Color of Teaching." *Journal of Teacher Education* 53, no. 2 (2002): 123–26.

Grant, Carl A., and Maureen Gillette. "A Candid Talk to Teacher Educators about Effectively Preparing Teachers Who Can Teach Everyone's Children." *Journal of Teacher Education* 57, no. 3 (May/June 2006): 292–99.

Haberman, Martin J. "The Preparation of Teachers for a Diverse, Free Society." Pp. 110–31 in *Teachers for the New Millennium: Aligning Teacher Development, National Goals, and High Standards for All Students,* edited by Leonard Kaplan and Roy Eldefelt. Thousand Oaks, CA: Corwin Press, 1996.

Hall, Budd. "Introduction." Pp. xiii–xxii in *Voices of Change: Participatory Research in the United States and Canada,* edited by Peter Park, Mary Brydon-Miller, Budd Hall, and Ted Jackson. Westport, CT: Bergin & Garvey, 1993.

Hamm, Deborah, David Dowell, and Jean W. Houck. "Service-Learning as a Strategy to Prepare Teacher Candidates for Contemporary Diverse Classrooms." *Education* 119, no. 2 (1998): 413–27.

Hartley, Matthew, Ira Harkavy, and Lee Benson. "Putting Down Roots in the Groves of Academe: The Challenges of Institutionalizing Service-Learning." Pp. 205–22 in *Service-Learning in Higher Education: Critical Issues and Directions*, edited by Dan W. Butin. New York: Palgrave Macmillan, 2005.

Harvey, Aminifu R. "An After-School Manhood Development Program." Pp. 157–68 in *Educating Our Black Children: New Directions and Radical Approaches*, edited by Richard Majors. New York: Routledge Falmer, 2001.

Harward, Donald W. "Engaged Learning and the Core Purposes of Liberal Education." *Liberal Education* 93, no. 1 (2007): 6–16.

Heath, Shirley Brice. "Island by Island We Must Cross: Challenges from Language and Culture Among African Americans." Pp. 163–86 in *African-Centered Schooling in Theory and Practice*, edited by Cheryl S. Ajirotutu and Diane S. Pollard. Westport, CT: Bergin & Garvey Publishers, Inc., 2000.

Heath, Shirley Brice, and Milbrey W. McLaughlin. "Community Organizations as Family: Endeavors That Engage and Support Adolescents." *Phi Delta Kappan* 72, no. 8 (1991): 623–27.

Hollins, Etta, and Maria Torres Guzman. "Research on Preparing Teachers for Diverse Populations." Pp. 477–548 in *Studying Teacher Education: The Report of the AERA Panel on Research and Teacher Education*, edited by Marilyn Cochran-Smith and Kenneth M. Zeichner. Mahwah, NJ: Lawrence Erlbaum Associates, 2005.

Holmes Group. *Tomorrow's Schools of Education*. East Lansing, MI: Author, 1995.

Holmes Partnership. "The Holmes Scholars." http://www.holmespartnership .org/scholars.html (accessed September 25, 2008).

Hoover, Mary Eleanor Rhodes. "The Nairobi Day School: An American Independent School, 1966–1984." *Journal of Negro Education* 61, no. 2 (1992): 201–10.

Howard, Tyrone C., and Glenda R. Aleman. "Teacher Capacity for Diverse Learners: What Do Teachers Need to Know?" Pp. 157–74 in *Handbook of Research on Teacher Education: Enduring Questions in Changing Contexts*, edited by Marilyn Cochran-Smith, Sharon Feiman-Nemser, D. John McIntyre, and Kelly Demers. New York: Routledge and Association of Teacher Educators, 2008.

Hoy, Ariane, and Wayne Meisel. *Civic Engagement at the Center: Building Democracy through Integrated Cocurricular and Curricular Experiences*. Washington, DC: The Association of American Colleges and Universities, 2008.

Hu, Kathyryn, and Karen Blake. "Cultural Identity and Learning to Teach in a Diverse Community: Findings from a Collective Case Study." *Journal of Teacher Education* 54, no. 3 (2003): 192–205.

Hyland, Nora E., and Susan E. Noffke. "Understanding Diversity through Social and Community Inquiry: An Action-Research Study." *Journal of Teacher Education*, 56 (September/October 2005): 367–81.

Imig, David G., and Scott R. Imig. "From Traditional Certification to Competitive Certification." Pp. 886–907 in *Handbook of Research on Teacher Education: Enduring Questions in Changing Contexts*, edited by Marilyn Cochran-Smith, Sharon Feiman-Nemser, D. John McIntyre, and Kelly Demers. New York: Routledge and Association of Teacher Educators, 2008.

Ingersoll, Richard M. "The Teacher Shortage: Myth or Reality?" *Educational Horizons* 81, no. 3 (2003): 146–52.

Interstate New Teacher Assessment and Support Consortium (INTASC). *Model Standards for Beginning Teacher Licensing, Assessment and Development: A Resource for State Dialogue.* Washington, DC: Author, 1992. http://www.ccsso.org/content/pdfs/corestrd.pdf (accessed September 18, 2008).

Irvine, Jacqueline Jordan. "Diversity and Teacher Education: People, Pedagogy, and Politics." Pp. 675–78 in *Handbook of Research on Teacher Education: Enduring Questions in Changing Contexts*, edited by Marilyn Cochran-Smith, Sharon Feiman-Nemser, D. John McIntyre, and Kelly Demers. New York: Routledge and Association of Teacher Educators, 2008.

———. *Educating Teachers for Diversity: Seeing with a Cultural Eye.* New York: Teachers College Press, 2003.

Jacoby, Barbara and Associates. *Building Partnerships for Service-Learning.* San Francisco: Jossey-Bass, 2003.

———. "Fundamentals of Service-Learning Partnerships." Pp. 1–19 in *Building Partnerships for Service-Learning*, edited by Barbara Jacoby and Associates. San Francisco: Jossey-Bass, 2003.

———. *Service-Learning in Higher Education: Concepts and Practices.* San Francisco: Jossey-Bass, 1996.

Kaplan, Leonard, and Roy Eldefelt. *Teachers for the New Millennium: Aligning Teacher Development, National Goals, and High Standards for All Students.* Thousand Oaks, CA: Corwin Press, 1996.

King, Joyce E., Etta R. Hollins, and Warren C. Hayman, eds. *Preparing Teachers for Cultural Diversity.* New York: Teachers College Press, 1997.

King, Joyce E., and Sharon Parker. "A Detroit Conversation." Pp. 243–60 in *Black Education: A Transformative Research and Action Agenda for the New Century*, edited by Joyce E. King. Mahwah, NJ: Lawrence Erlbaum Associates, 2005.

Klug, Beverly J., and Janice Hall. "Opening Doors to Wisdom: Working Together for Our Children." *Action in Teacher Education* 24, no. 2 (Summer 2002): 34–41.

Koerner, Mari, and Najwa Abdul-Tawwab. "Using Community as a Resource for Teacher Education: A Case Study." *Equity & Excellence in Education* 39, no. 1 (2006): 37–46.

Kravetz, Katherine. "Transforming Communities: The Role of Service Learning in a Community Studies Course." *International Journal of Teaching and Learning in Higher Education* 18, no. 1 (2006): 49–56.

Kreuger, Richard. *Analyzing and Reporting Focus Group Results.* Thousand Oaks, CA: Sage Publications, 1998.

Labaree, David F. "An Uneasy Relationship: The History of Teacher Education in the University." Pp. 290–306 in *Handbook of Research on Teacher Education: Enduring Questions in Changing Contexts*, edited by Marilyn Cochran-Smith, Sharon Feiman-Nemser, D. John McIntyre, and Kelly E. Demers. New York: Routledge and Association of Teacher Educators, 2008.

Ladson-Billings, Gloria. *Crossing Over to Canaan: The Journey of New Teachers in Diverse Classrooms.* San Francisco: Jossey-Bass, 2001.

———. "Culturally Relevant Pedagogy in African-Centered Schools: Possibilities for Progressive Educational Reform." Pp. 187–98 in *African-Centered Schooling in*

Theory and Practice, edited by Diane. S. Pollard and Cheryl. S. Ajirotutu. Westport, CT: Bergin & Garvey Publishers, Inc., 2000.

———. "Fighting for Our Lives: Preparing Teachers to Teach African American Students." *Journal of Teacher Education* 51, no. 3 (2000): 206–14.

———. "Toward a Theory of Culturally Relevant Pedagogy." *American Educational Research Journal* 32, no. 3 (1995): 465–91.

Lake, Vickie E., and Ithel Jones. "Service-Learning in Early Childhood Teacher Education: Using Service to Put Meaning Back into Learning." *Teaching and Teacher Education* 24, no. 8 (November 2008): 2146–56.

LaMothe, Roubbins Jamal. *Uncharted Territories: Past, Present, and Future.* Somerville, MA: Books of Hope Press, 2001.

Langseth, Mark. "Maximizing Impact, Minimizing Harm: Why Service-Learning Must More Fully Integrate Multicultural Education." Pp. 45–71 in *Integrating Service-Learning and Multicultural Education in Colleges and Universities*, edited by Carolyn R. O'Grady. Mahwah, NJ: Lawrence Erlbaum Associates, 2000.

Lee, Carol D. "The State of Knowledge about the Education of African Americans." Pp. 45–71 in *Black Education: A Transformative Research and Action Agenda for the New Century*, edited by Joyce E. King. Mahwah, NJ: Lawrence Erlbaum Associates, 2005.

Lesnick, Alice, Jody Cohen, and Alison Cook-Sather. "Working the Tensions: Constructing Educational Studies within a Traditional Liberal Arts Context." Pp. 54–79 in *Taking Teaching Seriously: How Liberal Arts Colleges Prepare Teachers to Meet Today's Educational Challenges*, edited by Christopher Bjork, D. Kay Johnston, and Heidi Ross. Boulder, CO: Paradigm Publishers, 2007.

Lewis, Tammy L. "Service Learning for Social Change? Lessons from a Liberal Arts College." *Teaching Sociology* 32, no. 1 (2004): 94–108.

Lisak-Shpak, Rivkah. *Pluralism & Progressives: Hull House and the New Immigrants, 1890–1919.* Chicago: University of Chicago Press, 1989.

Liston, Daniel Patrick, and Kenneth M. Zeichner. *Teacher Education and the Social Conditions of Schooling.* New York: Routledge, 1991.

Lucas, Tamara, and Jaime Grinberg. "Responding to the Linguistic Reality of Mainstream Classrooms: Preparing All Teachers to Teach English Language Learners." Pp. 606–36 in *Handbook of Research on Teacher Education: Enduring Questions in Changing Contexts*, edited by Marilyn Cochran-Smith, Sharon Feiman-Nemser, D. John McIntyre, and Kelly Demers. New York: Routledge and Association of Teacher Educators, 2008.

Mason, Sally Frost. "Do Colleges of Liberal Arts and Sciences Need Schools of Education?" *Educational Policy* 14, no. 121 (2000): 121–28.

Maurrasse, John. *Beyond the Campus: How Colleges and Universities Form Partnerships with Their Communities.* New York: Routledge, 2001.

McLaren, Peter, and Peter Leonard. *Paulo Freire: A Critical Encounter.* New York: Routledge, 1993.

Melnick, Susan L., and Kenneth M. Zeichner. "Teacher Education's Responsibility to Address Diversity Issues: Enhancing Institutional Capacity." *Theory into Practice* 37, no. 2 (1998): 88–95.

———. "Enhancing Capacity of Teacher Education Institutions to Address Diversity Issues." Pp. 23–39 in *Preparing Teachers for Cultural Diversity*, edited by Joyce

E. King, Etta R. Hollins, and Warren C. Hayman. New York: Teachers College Press, 1997.

Miles, Matthew B., and Michael A. Huberman. *Qualitative Data Analysis.* Thousand Oaks, CA: Sage Publications, 1994.

Minkler, Meredith, and Nina Wallerstein, eds. *Community-Based Participatory Research for Health.* San Francisco: Jossey-Bass, 2003.

Mule, Lucy. "Elucidating Barriers to Community Engagement: Literacy for a Healthier Community Partnership Project (2005–2007)." Unpublished report.

———. "Preservice Teachers' Inquiry in a Professional Development School Context: Implications for the Practicum." *Teaching and Teacher Education* 22, no. 2 (2006): 205–18.

Murrell, Peter C. Jr. *African-Centered Pedagogy: Developing Schools of Achievement for African American Children.* Albany: State University of New York Press, 2002.

———. *The Community Teacher: A New Framework for Effective Urban Teaching.* New York: Teachers College Press, 2001.

———. "The Education of Teachers: Ninety-Eighth Yearbook of the National Society for the Study of Education." *Journal of Teacher Education* 52, no. 1 (January 2001): 78.

———. "Toward Social Justice in Urban Education: A Model of Collaborative Cultural Inquiry in Urban Schools." *Equity & Excellence in Education* 39, no. 1 (2006): 81–90.

Myers, Carol, and Terry Pickeral. "Service-Learning: An Essential Process for Preparing Teachers as Transformational Leaders in the Reform of Public Education." Pp. 13–41 in *Learning with the Community: Concepts and Models for Service Learning in Teacher Education,* edited by Joseph Erickson and Jeffrey Anderson. Sterling, VA: Stylus Publishing, LLC, 2005.

National Comprehensive Center for Teacher Quality and Public Agenda. "Lessons Learned: New Teachers Talk About Their Jobs, Challenges and Long-Range Plans." 2008. http://www.publicagenda.org/reports/lessons-learned-new-teachers-talk-about-their-jobs-challenges-and-long-range-plans-issue-no-1 (accessed February 14, 2009).

National Council for Accreditation of Teacher Education (NCATE). Professional Standards for the Accreditation of Teacher Preparation Institutions. 2008. http://www.ncate.org/documents/standards/NCATE%20Standards%20 2008.pdf (accessed September 18, 2008).

Nieto, Sonia. *Affirming Diversity: The Sociopolitical Context of Multicultural Education.* New York: Longman, 2000.

———. "Bringing Bilingual Education Out of the Basement, and Other Imperatives for Teacher Education." Pp. 187–207 in *Lifting Every Voice: Pedagogy and Politics of Bilingualism,* edited by Zeynep F. Beykont. Cambridge, MA: Harvard Education Pub. Group, 2000.

———. "Placing Equity Front and Center: Some Thoughts on Transforming Teacher Education for a New Century." *Journal of Teacher Education* 51, no. 3 (2000): 180–87.

North End Campus Committee. "North End Campus Committee Resource Guide." Unpublished report, 2007.

Nyden, Philip. "Partnerships for Collaborative Action Research." Pp. 213–23 in *Building Partnerships for Service-Learning*, edited by Barbara Jacoby and Associates. San Francisco: Jossey-Bass, 2003.

Nygreen, Kysa, Soo Ah Kwon, and Patricia Sánchez. "Urban Youth Building Community: Social Change and Participatory Research in Schools, Homes, and Community-Based Organizations." *Journal of Community Practice* 14, no. 1 and 2 (September 2006): 107–23.

O'Grady, Carolyn R., ed. *Integrating Service-Learning and Multicultural Education in Colleges and Universities*. Mahwah, NJ: Lawrence Erlbaum Associates, 2000.

O'Meara, KerryAnn. "Encouraging Multiple Forms of Scholarship in Faculty Reward Systems: Does It Make a Difference?" *Research in Higher Education* 46, no. 5 (2005): 479–510.

———. "Reframing Incentives and Rewards for Community Service-Learning and Academic Outreach." *Journal of Higher Education Outreach and Engagement* 8, no. 2 (2003): 201–20.

O'Meara, KerryAnn, and Eugene R. Rice, eds. *Faculty Priorities Reconsidered: Rewarding Multiple Forms of Scholarship*. San Francisco: Jossey-Bass, 2005.

Orfield, Gary, ed. *Dropouts in America: Confronting the Graduation Rate Crisis*. Cambridge, MA: Harvard Education Press, 2004.

Pascarella, Ernest T., Gregory C. Wolniak, Ty M. Cruce, and Charles F. Blaich. *ASHE Higher Education Report* 31, no. 3 (2005): 1–23.

———. "Do Liberal Arts Colleges Really Foster Good Practices in Undergraduate Education?" *Journal of College Student Development* 45, no. 1 (2004): 57–74.

Patton, Michael Q. *Quantitative Evaluation and Research Methods*. Thousand Oaks, CA: Sage Publications, 1990.

Percy, Stephen L., Nancy Zimpher, and Mary Jane Brukardt, eds. *Creating a New Kind of University: Institutionalizing Community-University Engagement*. Bolton, MA: Anker Publishing Company, 2006.

Perl, Sondra, Beth Counihan, Tim McCormack, and Emily Schnee. "Storytelling as Scholarship: A Writerly Approach to Research." *English Education* 39, no. 4 (2007): 306–25.

Pollard, Diane S., and Cheryl S. Ajirotutu. *African-Centered Schooling in Theory and Practice*. Westport, CT: Bergin & Garvey Publishers, Inc., 2000.

Prince, Gregory. "A Liberal Arts College Perspective." Pp. 249–62 in *Civic Responsibility and Higher Education*, edited by Thomas Ehrlich. Phoenix, AZ: Oryx Press, 2000.

Quiocho, Alice, and Francisco Rios. "The Power of Their Presence: Minority Group Teachers and Schooling." *Review of Educational Research* 70, no. 4 (2000): 485–528.

Reardon, Kenneth M. "Participatory Action Research as Service Learning." *New Directions for Teaching and Learning* 73 (1998): 57–64.

Rhoads, Robert A. "How Civic Engagement Is Reframing Liberal Education." *Liberal Education* (spring 2003): 25–28.

Rhoads, Robert A., and Jeffrey P. F. Howard, eds. *Academic Service Learning: A Pedagogy of Action and Reflection*. San Francisco: Jossey-Bass, 1998.

Royster, Jacqueline Jones. *Traces of a Stream: Literacy and Social Change among African American Women*. Pittsburgh, PA: University of Pittsburgh Press, 2000.

Sarason, Seymour. *The Case for Change: Rethinking the Preparation of Educators*. San Francisco: Jossey-Bass, 1993.

Sax, Linda. "Citizenship Development and the American College Student." Pp. 3–18 in *Civic Responsibility and Higher Education*, edited by Thomas Ehrlich. Phoenix, AZ: Oryx Press, 2000.

Schlechty, Phillip C., and Victor S. Vance, "Recruitment, Selection, and Retention: The Shape of the Teaching Force." *The Elementary School Journal* 83, no. 4 (March 1983): 469–87.

Shulman, Lee S. "Knowledge and Teaching: Foundations of the New Reform." *Harvard Educational Review* (February 1987): 1–22.

Schultz, Brian D. "Not Satisfied with Stupid Band-Aids": A Portrait of a Justice-Oriented, Democratic Curriculum Serving a Disadvantaged Neighborhood." *Equity & Excellence in Education* 40 (2007): 166–76.

Sconzert, Karen, Demetria Iazetto, and Stewart Purkey. "Small-Town College to Big-City School: Preparing Urban Teachers from Liberal Arts Colleges." *Teaching and Teacher Education* 16, no. 4 (2000): 465–90.

Seidl, Barbara. "Working with Communities to Explore and Personalize Culturally Relevant Pedagogies: 'Push, Double Images, and Raced Talk.'" *Journal of Teacher Education* 58, no. 2 (2007): 168–83.

Seidl, Barbara, and Gloria Friend. "Unification of Church and State: Universities and Churches Working Together to Nurture Anti-Racist, Biculturally Competent Teachers." *Journal of Teacher Education* 53, no. 2 (2002a): 142–52.

———. "Leaving Authority at the Door: Equal Status Community-Based Experiences and the Preparation of Teachers for Diverse Classrooms." *Teaching and Teacher Education* 18, no. 4 (2002b): 421–33.

Shirley, Dennis, Afra Hersi, Elizabeth MacDonald, Maria Sanchez, Connie Scandone, Charles Skidmore, and Patrick Tutwiler. "Bringing the Community Back In: Change, Accommodation, and Contestation in a School University Partnership." *Equity & Excellence in Education* 39 (2006): 27–36.

Shor, Ira, and Paulo Freire. *A Pedagogy for Liberation: Dialogues on Transforming Education*. Granby, MA: Bergin & Garvey Publishers, Inc., 1987.

Silva, Cynthia M., Robert P. Moses, Parker Johnson, and Jacqueline Rivers. "The Algebra Project: Making School Mathematics Count." *Journal of Negro Education* 59, no. 3 (1990): 375–91.

Sleeter, Christine. "Equity, Democracy, and Neoliberal Assaults on Teacher Education." *Teaching and Teacher Education* 24 (2008): 1947–57.

———. "An Invitation to Support Diverse Students through Teacher Education." *Journal of Teacher Education* 59, no. 3 (2008): 212–19.

———. *Multicultural Education as Social Activism*. Albany, NY: State University of New York Press, 1996.

———. "Preparing Teachers for Culturally Diverse Schools: Research and the Overwhelming Presence of Whiteness." *Journal of Teacher Education* 52 (2001): 94–106.

———. "Preparing White Teachers for Diverse Students." Pp. 551–58 in *Handbook of Research on Teacher Education: Enduring Questions in Changing Contexts*, edited by Marilyn Cochran-Smith, Sharon Feiman-Nemser, D. John McIntyre, and

Kelly Demers. New York: Routledge and Association of Teacher Educators, 2008.

———. "Strengthening Multicultural Education with Community-Based Learning." Pp. 263–76 in *Integrating Service-Learning and Multicultural Education in Colleges and Universities*, edited by Carolyn R. O'Grady. Mahwah, NJ: Lawrence Erlbaum Associates, 2000.

Smith College Office of Educational Outreach. www.smith.edu/outreach/partnerships_gerena.php (accessed January 20, 2008).

Smulyan, Lisa. "'The Power of a Teacher': Teacher Education for Social Justice." Pp. 80–99 in *Taking Teaching Seriously: How Liberal Arts Colleges Prepare Teachers to Meet Today's Educational Challenges*, edited by Christopher Bjork, D. Kay Johnston, and Heidi Ross. Boulder, CO: Paradigm Publishers, 2007.

Speck, Bruce W., and Sherry L. Hoppe, eds. *Service-Learning: History, Theory, and Issues*. Westport: Praeger, 2004.

Stachowski, Laura L., and Christopher J. Frey. "Lessons Learned in Navajoland: Student Teachers Reflect on Professional and Cultural Learning in Reservation Schools and Communities." *Action in Teacher Education* 25, no. 3 (2003): 38–47.

Stachowski, Laura, and James M. Mahan. "Cross-Cultural Field Placements: Student Teachers Learning from Schools and Communities." *Theory into Practice* 37, no. 2 (1998): 154–62.

Stachowski, Laura, Jayson Richardson, and Michelle Henderson. "Student Teachers Report on the Influence of Cultural Values on Classroom Practice and Community Involvement: Perspectives from the Navajo Reservation and from Abroad." *Teacher Educator* 39, no. 1 (2003): 52–63.

Stoecker, Randy. *Research Methods for Community Change: A Project-Based Approach*. Thousand Oaks, CA: Sage Publications, 2005.

Strand, Kerry J., Nicholas Cutforth, Randy Stoecker, Sam Marullo, and Patrick Donohue. *Community-Based Research and Higher Education: Principles and Practices*. San Francisco: Jossey-Bass, 2003.

Teitel, Lee. *The Professional Development Schools Handbook: Starting, Sustaining, and Assessing Partnerships That Improve Student Learning*. Thousand Oaks, CA: Corwin Press, 2003.

Terill, Marguerite, and Diane L. Mark. "Preservice Teachers' Expectations for Schools with Children of Color and Second-Language Learners." *Journal of Teacher Education* 51, no. 2 (2000): 149–55.

Terry, Alice, and Jahn Bohnenberger. *Service-Learning by Degrees: How Adolescents Can Make a Difference in the Real World*. Portsmouth, NH: Heinemann, 2007.

Thomas, Nancy L. (2000). "The College and University as Citizen." Pp. 63–97 in *Civic Responsibility and Higher Education*, edited by Thomas Ehrlich. Phoenix, AZ: Oryx Press, 2000.

Thompson, Gail L. *Through Ebony Eyes*. San Francisco: Jossey-Bass, 2004.

———. *What African American Parents Want Educators to Know*. Westport, CT: Praeger, 2003.

Tiezzi, Linda J., and Beverly E. Cross. "Utilizing Research on Prospective Teachers' Beliefs to Inform Urban Field Experiences." *Urban Review* 29, no. 2 (1997): 113–25.

Timmermans, Steven R., and Jeffrey P. Bouman. "Seven Ways of Teaching and Learning: University-Community Partnerships at Baccalaureate Institutions." *Journal of Community Practice* 12, nos. 3 and 4 (2005): 89–101.

Trumbull, Elise, Carrie Rothstein-Fisch, Patricia M Greenfield, and Blanca Quiroz. *Bridging Cultures Between Home and School: A Guide for Teachers.* Mahwah, NJ: Lawrence Erlbaum Associates, 2001.

University Community Partnerships-Current Practices. 1999. http://www.oup .org/files/pubs/currentpractices3.pdf (accessed June 5, 2008).

Verducci, Susan, and Denise Pope. "Rationales for Integrating Service-Learning in Teacher Education." Pp. 2–18 in *Service-Learning in Teacher Education: Enhancing the Growth of New Teachers, Their Students, and Communities*, edited by Jeffrey B. Anderson, Kevin J. Swick and Joost Yff. Washington, DC: American Association of Colleges for Teacher Education (AACTE), 2001

Villegas, Ana María, and Danné E. Davis."Preparing Teachers of Color to Confront Racial/Ethnic Disparities in Educational Outcomes." Pp. 583–605 in *Handbook of Research on Teacher Education: Enduring Questions in Changing Contexts*, edited by Marilyn Cochran-Smith, Sharon Feiman-Nemser, D. John McIntyre, and Kelly Demers. New York: Routledge and Association of Teacher Educators, 2008.

Villegas, Ana María, and Tamara Lucas. *Educating Culturally Responsive Teachers: A Coherent Approach.* Albany: State University of New York Press, 2002.

Wade, Rahima. C. "Service-Learning for Social Justice in the Elementary Classroom: Can We Get There from Here?" *Equity & Excellence in Education* 40 (2007): 156–65.

Wade, Rahima C., Jeffrey B. Anderson, Donald B. Yarbrough, Terry Pickeral, Joseph B. Erickson, and Thomas Kromer. "Novice Teachers' Experiences of Community Service–Learning." *Teaching and Teacher Education* 15, no. 6 (1999): 667–84.

Wanat, John. "Weaving Engagement into the Fabric of Campus Administration." Pp. 212–22 in *Creating a New Kind of University: Institutionalizing Community-University Engagement*, edited by Stephen Percy, Nancy Zimpher, and Mary Jane Brukardt. Bolton, MA: Anker Publishing Company, Inc., 2006.

Ward, Kelly, and Lisa Wolf-Wendel. "Community-Centered Service Learning: Moving from Doing for to Doing With." *American Behavioral Scientist* 43, no. 5 (2000): 767–80.

Warfield-Coppock, Nsenga. "The Rites of Passage Movement: A Resurgence of African-Centered Practices for Socializing African American Youth." *Journal of Negro Education* 61, no. 4 (1992): 471–82.

Westheimer, Joel. "Politics and Patriotism in Education." *Phi Delta Kappan* 87, no. 8 (2006): 607–20.

Wiggins, Robert A., Eric J. Follo, and Mary B. Eberly. "The Impact of a Field Immersion Program on Pre-Service Teachers' Attitudes toward Teaching in Culturally Diverse Classrooms." *Teaching and Teacher Education* 23 (2007): 653–63.

Williams, Boyce C., ed. *Reforming Teacher Education through Accreditation: Telling Our Story.* Washington, DC: National Council for Accreditation of Teacher Education, 2000.

Williams, Heather A. *Self-Taught: African American Education in Slavery and Freedom*. Chapel Hill: University of North Carolina Press, 2005.

Zeichner, Kenneth M. "The Adequacies and Inadequacies of Three Current Strategies to Recruit, Prepare, and Retain the Best Teachers for All Students." *Teachers College Record* 105, no. 3 (2003): 490–519.

———. "Introduction: Settings for Teacher Education" Pp. 263–68 in *Handbook of Research on Teacher Education: Enduring Questions in Changing Contexts*, edited by Marilyn Cochran-Smith, Sharon Feiman-Nemser, D. John McIntyre, and Kelly Demers. New York: Routledge and Association of Teacher Educators, 2008.

———. "Reflections of a University-Based Teacher Educator on the Future of College- and University-Based Teacher Education." *Journal of Teacher Education* 57, no. 3 (2006): 326–40.

———. *Teacher Education and the Struggle for Social Justice*. New York: Routledge, 2009.

Zeichner, Ken M., and Karen Hoeft. "Teacher Socialization for Cultural Diversity." Pp. 525–47 in *Handbook of Research on Teacher Education*, 3rd ed., edited by John P. Sikula, Thomas J. Buttery, and Edith Guyton. New York: Macmillan, 1996.

Zeichner, Ken M., and Susan L. Melnick. "The Role of Community Field Experiences in Preparing Teachers for Cultural Diversity." Pp. 176–96 in *Currents of Reform in Preservice Teacher Education*, edited by Ken Zeichner, Susan Melnick, and Mary Louise Gomez. New York: Teachers College Press, 1996.

Zeichner, Ken, Susan Melnick, and Mary Louise Gomez, eds. *Currents of Reform in Preservice Teacher Education*. New York: Teachers College Press, 1996.

Zimpher, Nancy L. "Right-Sizing Teacher Education: The Policy Imperative." Pp. 43–62 in *Teachers for the New Millennium: Aligning Teacher Development, National Goals, and High Standards for All Students*, edited by Leonard Kaplan and Roy A. Edelfelt. Thousand Oaks, CA: Corwin Press, 1996.

Zumwalt, Karen, and Elizabeth Craig. "Who Is Teaching? Does It Matter?" Pp. 404–24 in *Handbook of Research on Teacher Education: Enduring Questions in Changing Contexts*, edited by Marilyn Cochran-Smith, Sharon Feiman-Nemser, D. John McIntyre, and Kelly Demers. New York: Routledge and Association of Teacher Educators, 2008.

Index

About the Author

Lucy W. Mule is associate professor in the Department of Education and Child Study and the faculty co-director of the Center for Community Collaboration at Smith College. She teaches courses in multicultural education, comparative education, literacy in cross-cultural perspective, and methods of instruction. Her current research interests include college-community partnerships, community service-learning, and multicultural teacher education. Lucy has written articles on teacher education reform in *Teaching and Teacher Education*, *Teacher Education and Practice*, and *Electronic Magazine for Multicultural Education*. She has contributed book chapters to *African Americans and Community Engagement in Higher Education*, *The Structure and Agency of Women's Education*, and *What Is Indigenous Knowledge? Voices from the Academy*.

Breinigsville, PA USA
09 June 2010
239456BV00001B/8/P